STRAIGHT WIVES, SHATTERED LIVES VOLUME 3

True Stories of Women Married to Gay & Bisexual Men

Compiled and Edited by

BONNIE KAYE, M.Ed.

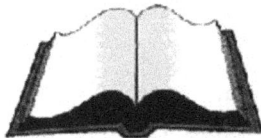

CCB Publishing
British Columbia, Canada

Straight Wives, Shattered Lives Volume 3:
True Stories of Women Married to Gay & Bisexual Men

Copyright © 2020 by Bonnie Kaye, M.Ed.
ISBN-13: 978-1-77143-460-7
First Edition

Library and Archives Canada Cataloguing in Publication
Title: Straight wives, shattered lives. Volume 3 : true stories of women
married to gay & bisexual men / compiled and edited by Bonnie Kaye.
Other titles: Straight wives. Volume 3 | True stories of women married to
gay & bisexual men | True stories of women married to gay and bisexual men
Names: Kaye, Bonnie, 1951- editor.
Description: First edition. | Volumes 1 and 2 published under title: Straight wives.
Identifiers: Canadiana (print) 20200411365 | Canadiana (ebook) 20200412051
| ISBN 9781771434607 (softcover) | ISBN 9781771434614 (PDF)
Subjects: LCSH: Bisexuality in marriage.
| LCSH: Gay men—Relations with heterosexual women.
| LCSH: Closeted gays—Family relationships. | LCSH: Marital conflict.
| LCSH: Husbands—Sexual behavior. | LCSH: Wives—Biography.
Classification: LCC HQ1035 .S774 2020 | DDC 306.872—dc23

Front Cover is an original work of art by Heather Pettersen:
Facebook: https://www.facebook.com/heather.pettersen
Instagram: https://www.instagram.com/heatherpettersen

Publisher: CCB Publishing
               British Columbia, Canada
               www.ccbpublishing.com

Dedication

This book is dedicated to the women in my support network who continually amaze me with their kindness, strength, humor, and compassion.

It is also dedicated to Heather Pettersen, my friend who painted the beautiful cover artwork for this book. Heather led me into the light during a very dark period of time with my gay ex-husband. She truly changed my life for the better and has never stopped. I love you Heather!

Other books by Bonnie Kaye

The Gay Husband Checklist for Women Who Wonder

Over the Cliff: Gay Husbands in Straight Marriages

Doomed Grooms: Gay Husbands of Straight Wives

Man Readers: A Woman's Guide to Dysfunctional Men

Straight Wives, Shattered Lives (Volume 1)

Straight Wives, Shattered Lives (Volume 2)

Bonnie Kaye's Straight Talk

How I Made My Husband Gay: Myths About Straight Wives

Gay Husbands Say the Darndest Things

Jennifer Needle in Her Arm

and

La Lista de Control para Esposos Gay
Y Para Mujeres Que se Preguntan

Spanish edition of
The Gay Husband Checklist for Women Who Wonder

Contents

Introduction

Fifteen years ago, I published the book **Straight Wives, Shattered Lives**. Five years later, a second edition was published. I was so grateful for the many women who were willing to share their experiences of living through this nightmare and the long-term painful effects they lived with for many years later. These "scabs" are caused by the scars of being in an abusive marriage to a gay man. For those women who are desperate to make a connection to others living this hell, these two books are truly inspirational and helpful. I still receive letters every week from women thanking me for the stories that our women shared. Thousands of women who read these books felt an immediate connection to a stranger from a different place, space, culture, or religion. It's as if you are reliving your life through the eyes of others who really GET IT. Yes, I say GET IT because unless you have lived this life and walked in these shoes, you just don't really understand.

The women who contribute these stories are not looking for revenge or to punish their gay husbands. Rather they are telling their truths to share this unique experience with others so they will know they are not alone. Although we are living in a very different generation than the years when I first started my support system in 1982, the problem still exists—and in some ways, it is worse.

That may surprise you in view of the new liberal attitudes of society that is far more open about homosexuality. In the last decade, gay marriage has become legal. Gay people no longer have to hide inside a "closet" pretending to be straight. They don't have to marry women to conceal their secret. They can attend gay pride parades and not cover their faces in fear of being exposed.

So what's the "worse" part? That is the part that our straight wives have to endure when their husbands come out and become the new *heroes*. Now society sings praises to these men who have the courage to live their new "authentic lives." They cheer them on. They feel saddened over the years of *torture* they had to endure by pretending they were "straight men." They want to pin a big round badge of COURAGE button on their shirts. In the past, women would at least get some sympathy from their friends and acquaintances. Not now—now our gay husbands are getting that misplaced sympathy. Society sees them as the victims—rather than us. **That has changed**—and it doesn't help us.

In the past, we'd get some snickers and sneers from people with the usual, "You didn't know he was gay when you married him? It's so obvious," or "Was he gay when you married him?" Yes, those were the usual passive-aggressive comments we would hear as if we had missed the boat. Or they thought maybe we did know—but we were desperate. Sadly, that's how ignorance thinks.

But back then—after the little slap down of accusation, we would be lifted up like a wine glass with some words of comfort including, "That's so terrible. How could he do that to you?" Yep, those words would take away the sting of the initial slap in the face with a few soothing words.

Well, I don't hear those words very much anymore. People don't sympathize with us—the true victims of this situation. And that is what has changed the most. They are so impressed with these gay men who spent 20, 30, 40, and more years of their lives living their lies with us—their loving (although confused) wives giving up what these men claim were the "best years of their lives to their families." So now that their dues have been paid, it is time for them treat themselves to authenticity in a world where they always belonged. Yep, they are the new heroes for their bravery. People applaud them for staying in their marriages until the children were grown and on their own.

So, in other words, these men spent a few decades living a daily lie with their family. They were gay men playing the role of straight husbands. And yes, I mean playing a role. Gay men are not straight. They learn to "imitate" the actions of straight men. They study their body action, walk, arm motions, their speech, and heterosexual interests the same way that an actor prepares for a role. They usually have a lot of material to draw from via their family and friends. I always use the example of the comedian Lily Tomlin who is in the sitcom Frankie and Grace. Tomlin plays the role of a straight wife who in later life learns her husband is gay. She plays the role very well—because that's what it is—a role. Tomlin is a lesbian who is honest about her sexuality. And yet, she is also an excellent actress who can portray a straight wife. That is different than being in a relationship with a partner. Then she would be in the same position as our gay husbands trying to figure out how not to get caught.

When most of our husbands were growing up, gay was taboo. Being straight was a requirement. "Practicing straight" was a daily job—and these guys learned how to imitate and play the role. In fact in many cases, they went beyond normal "straight behaviors." Self-loathing often translated into anti-gay sentiments that these guys dropped in their conversations with straight people. My ex-husband would mock gay men who were effeminate calling them insulting names. He wasn't "that kind of gay" as if it would make him less gay.

When people ask our women, "Didn't you know he was gay when you married him," the answer is a resounding NO. How would we know? My gay husband was a kung fu teacher who was tall, handsome, and muscular. Women fell for him fast and easy. He was the epitome of a macho athlete. Why would gay even enter into my mind? Gay men wanted men, not women, right? Why would a gay man romance me, claim to fall in love with me, make love to me (have sex with me) and want to marry me? That's not what a gay man is supposed to do. But who knew? Not me. Not us.

I grew up in the 1960's and 1970's. Back in those days, sexuality was explored in new ways than in the past. It was not unusual to hear the term "experimentation" when you talked to some people. I've stated in other books I've written about a relationship I had in my 20's with a high school boyfriend. We went our separate ways for five years and reunited when I was 26 and living in New York. We spent our first evening back together talking about our past five years. I had been through a bad marriage. He had been through four relationships. He was very honest when he told me that two of them were with men. It did surprise me, but he assured me that he knew at this point that he was straight. He tried it, didn't like it, and abandoned it. Guess what? It sounded logical to me, and so we continued dating. It fizzled out because I knew something was off—but I never attributed it to GAY. I thought it was because he was a Cancer on the astrological sign. That's how stupid we used to be. In later years, he came to terms with his homosexuality and partnered with a man.

When gay men are young, some of them can pull off having sex with their wives. They know something is not quite right, but they do *try* to enjoy it. Some of them even try to get their wives to enjoy it. But in almost all cases, that sexual enjoyment starts to fade within a short amount of time. This is when the games begin. In time, a gay man just can't get himself to perform sex with his wife. He can't find the excitement, and in time that initial "excitement" turns to "revulsion." They don't have the desire for their wives that a straight man would have—because they can't. In almost every situation, the sexual activity in these marriages starts going downhill within a short amount of time.

Now, instead of just being honest and saying that **he** has a problem, the gay husband will go out of his way to make sure that his wife is the one who has the problem. He will do everything he can to discourage her from wanting to have sex. A dozen years ago, I wrote a column in one of my newsletters for Valentine's Day using a parody from the Paul Simon song **50 Ways To Leave Your Lover**. It stated:

Here's the funny thing—as much as you are thinking about sex, so is your gay husband. You are thinking about how you can get him to be intimate with you, while he is thinking about how to say NO to you. Remember that song **50 Ways to Leave Your Lover** *by Paul Simon? You know the one that says, "Get off the bus, Gus. Make a new plan, Stan. No need to be coy, Roy." Yep, for your gay husband, it's* **50 Ways to Say No to Your Wife**. *It could include lyrics like: "I've got a new pain, Jane. I have too much stress, Bess. You're much too large, Marge. I need some air, Clair. My tooth does hurt, Gert. There's a pain in my head, Peg." Yep, I bet I could rewrite that song in a flash. Sadly, so could all of you.*

Marriages to gay men are totally different than straight men. In a straight marriage, two people can grow apart and no longer want to be together. They go on their way after grieving the marriage and often feel the need to meet someone else. Many straight marriages don't work out because people married young; they grew in different directions, and no longer wanted to be together. This is not to say that there aren't straight men with all different kinds of personality disorders—because there are. But no matter how bad a straight husband is, at least he was straight. He wasn't sexually rejecting you and taking away your sense of feminine spirit. Yes, this is what a gay husband will do— take away your feelings of well-being in the bedroom.

People say that sex doesn't take that much time in a marriage, and after a number of years, the sexual activity lessens. But when it does lessen, it's not because of sexual rejection—but rather circumstances. It could be children, work, finances, depression, and other day-to-day pressures. At least it didn't start out that way. However, with a gay husband, it's **humiliating**. No woman wants to continually pursue her husband to have sex with her. And when the 50 excuses run out, he turns his anger on you. You are boring in bed, you have bad breath, you're too fat, you're too thin, you smell. Rather than be humiliated further, you just stop asking. Then he says you never make a move. Of course. It's degrading. And if you make a move? He pulls an excuse out of his hat.

Many of my women vow to live their lives alone after these marriages, never wanting to find a man again. They have lost the faith in themselves of trusting someone again. That seems to be the biggest fear of all—trusting again. When you have devoted decades of your life to men who lied to you and cheated on you, trust does come hard. When you read these stories, you will understand why.

The women who volunteered to share their stories with you are from my online support group. They come from all over the world including Pakistan, the Netherlands, the United Kingdom, and Canada. Most of them have never met personally; however, they all feel a kinship to each other as if they are sisters. They are sisters in pain, and their support for each other is always there. They are always willing to lend a shoulder to anyone in need of help and support. I hope you learn from their stories that you are not alone.

Sue's Story

I had a high school boyfriend who I married at the age of 21, right before I graduated from college. We had two children in very short order, and we experienced life events that unfortunately led to our divorce five years later. During the next nine years I dated many men who, without exception, would break up with me without notice, having already strayed with another woman. I sought therapy, and after describing these men in great detail, I was told each was a narcissist, and because of my trusting nature, they would destroy me. I should ultimately be with a reliable and steady man, but he might not necessarily be the most good looking or sexually attractive, and in fact I might actually find him boring, but to not let it stop me.

I was working hard at my career and raising my two children, and I decided to not even look for someone any longer, but rather to just go about my life and let the chips fall where they may. Fast forward a few years, I found myself and several coworkers taking a weekend girls trip to a coastal area in California. We went out on a Friday night, and our girls' table was seated right next to a group of men together doing pretty much the same thing. Our two tables ended up connecting, and I immediately noticed a cute, somewhat nerdy guy that I instantaneously liked. After socializing for a bit, we joined them at a beach house, where "Matt" and I connected, and the night ended with him kissing me and asking for my phone number. As it turns out, we both were from the same city in California, and after no more than ten minutes on my drive home at the end of the weekend, he was calling me and we arranged for him to come over for a visit that very night.

We were a couple from that point forward, but did not sleep together for several weeks. When we did, it was nice, but it lacked the sexual passion I had previously experienced. I vividly remembered thinking in that first encounter that this was what the therapist from years prior had talked about, that the "good guy" might be a bit dull, even boring, but good for me.

Sixteen months later we got married in a big church ceremony. The kiss at the altar was awkward. I kissed him, but he did not kiss me, he just stood there with his arms at his side. On our wedding night, as we were going to bed, in what I thought at the time was just a kidding-around moment, he said, "Well, I guess we're supposed to have sex on our wedding night, so let's get this over with!"

I noticed things, such as him not looking at women the way a man might. He never once told me I was pretty or complimented me physically, even though I had plenty of other men who did. I spied obvious gay men looking at him, following him. When I asked Matt if he was a leg man or a breast man, he said, "Oh, nothing really." I had sexy lingerie from a bridal shower, and he told me I should go ahead and return it and get myself something comfortable since he "Wasn't into it."

Fast forward two years, he wasn't initiating sex any longer. At this point, he was only 28 years old. He and I had started what would be another thirteen years of discussions as to why we did not have a regular sex life. At one point, we went two and a half years with no sex at all. These discussions would range from a brief mild talk to downright raised-voice fights. This is how it would go:

Me: Why aren't we having sex?

Him: I don't know.

Me: Are you interested in sex?

Him: Of course.

Me: Then why aren't we having sex?

Him: I don't know.

Me: Anybody and everybody would know why they don't want to have sex, why don't you?

Him: I don't know.

Me: Are you not attracted to me?

Him: You are a very attractive woman. (Notice the lack of actually answering the question?)

Me: Were you molested as a child?

Him: No.

Me: Were you taught that sex was dirty, or feel ashamed about your body?

Him: No.

Me: Are you gay?

Him: No.

Me: Do you masturbate?

Him: No.

Me: Well none of this makes sense, why aren't we having sex then?

Him: I don't know.

Me: Are you aware that when you don't tell me what is going on that I have nowhere else to go but to blame myself, that there is something wrong with me?

Him: No response at all.

He was a triathlete, and at one point I convinced him to get testosterone supplements that might help, and it was the only thing he was willing to try. He later told me in one fight the only reason he agreed to this was because he thought it would make him a better athlete. By the way, the only hair left unshaved on his body was his head.

We began to have constant arguments because where he said he was going to go was not where he actually went. He would claim that I wasn't remembering correctly. I felt like I had to walk around recording every conversation, because he would change is story. "But Matt, that's not what you said," became a theme. I learned later this is a real thing called gaslighting, but at the time he wanted me to think I was crazy and losing my mind. I would walk past his home office, and he would immediately click out of whatever he was looking at on the computer and go to another screen. He was obsessed with Men's Health magazines and had photos of men torn out of them stuffed into his nightstand. When I asked him why, he said he was saving them because they had recipes on the back (he didn't cook) or workout regimens (they had ads). He would spend a lot of time with specific running or cycling "buddies," and speak about them the way a 15 year old girl would about a boy she has a crush on.

I knew something was wrong, was very desperately "off," and in a big way. I tried for years to engage him, and he would not engage back. I had to beg for affection and had to ask for permission to kiss him goodbye in the morning. Besides feeling very bad about myself, I felt an overwhelming oppressing sense of doom that I did not know where it was coming from or what that doom was going to be or when. I got to the point where I felt a sense a hopelessness that is difficult to put into words. It would loom over me at all times. At several points, I thought that maybe it would easier to just not be alive as I already felt I was dead inside. Everything I did was "going through the motions." I felt trapped, defeated, exhausted, and lost.

We had one last big sex discussion, and it was the first time I completely lost it. I screamed at him that I knew he had been lying to me our entire marriage, and I was going to make it my mission to find out everything. Four days later, we had a normal night, with a normal dinner, went to bed just like we always do. The next morning he woke me up and said, verbatim, "When I go to work today, I won't be coming home. I want a divorce and we are not going to discuss it."

I asked him why, and he said, "You are not supportive of my running and you don't like motorsports." Yes, he actually said that, after 15 years of marriage at that point. He left, taking just his sporting equipment, and he cherry-picked through his clothes and left then rest. He moved in with a guy he refused to identify.

I found a therapist, and I was able to drag him along for a few sessions, and after the fourth, the therapist told Matt he had never seen a more narcissistic or immature man in 35 years of his work with couples, and he knew he was being lied to about everything we had discussed. He said when we came back for the next session we were going to have to focus on him and his dishonesty. Matt never went back and actually left me a note on the kitchen counter that he wasn't going back because he "didn't want to give me hope when there was none." As excruciating as that was to read, I believe it might have been the only honest thing he said to me during our entire marriage.

I knew it was directly related to his sexuality. I spoke with his brother, and the brother had found a stack of Playgirl magazines in his bedroom when they were back in high school, which Matt (laughingly) defended by saying he was writing a paper for school. My super sleuth girlfriend found he was following gay porn sites, including one that was focused on clean-shaven teenage boys, and others that sell sex toys for gay men to have sex with each other. My younger sister told me she thought he was gay before we got married, but I "seemed so happy" so she didn't say anything. Others sensed he was gay but thought "we had an arrangement." A former co-worker of my ex said he was surprised when we got engaged because he always thought Matt was gay, but like most people, thought he misjudged his sexuality because he was getting married to a woman.

On the two occasions that Matt came back to the house after he was gone, I repeatedly asked why he had left so abruptly. All he would say was that he had it planned for years but would refuse to give a reason as to why. I finally asked him "Is it because of all the fights we had had about sex?" His one and only close-to-admission answer was, "You had reason." I knew definitively in that moment that I was right all along--that I had been living a life of fraud.

The pain and devastation I experienced was overwhelming. I was not able to eat properly for almost a year, and I almost ended up in the hospital. I spent six years in therapy, went through EMDR treatment, tried at least seven different anti-depression meds, read a stack of books 20 feet high, and spent thousands on workshops and self-help programs. I even went to a psychiatrist to see if there was a way through shock therapy or some other means he could reprogram my brain to wipe out all memory of Matt and this experience. I would have tried anything to get out of the debilitating pain. It had been a slow drip of emotional torture which left me with no self-esteem, and I do not see the world in the same way. I have no idea who is telling the truth about anything. It has now been almost ten years, and I still struggle daily.

I received no truth, no admission, no discussion of what really happened -- no apology, no concern, no care, no closure. I was simply discarded. He turned out to be a sociopath, I did not matter one iota, and I am left to grapple with that for the rest of my life.

Megan's Story

I was married to my husband for twenty years when my world and my family came crashing down in a Tsunami of lies. My discovery was triggered upon reading an obscure text between my gay ex-husband (GEX) and a guy from the local gym at 4:30 a.m. I could not believe what I was reading, nor did I really understand the terminology until I did some google research. At first the dialogue between my ex and this stranger made no sense; I learned quickly, however, it was sexual references, and the relationship went back for quite some time.

This was a shock. We had been going to some counseling, and the conversations were always about working things out. The marriage had been rocky for a while, but I could not pin-point why. There was lots of screaming and arguing. Everything was always my fault. I tried hard to accommodate him. GEX was a very confused, mentally unstable individual. He would throw tantrums. I was always the facilitator – trying to make things work so as to minimize his outbursts.

I needed to get my facts straight, and this was the week before Christmas. I had to remain calm and wait until I got my boys back from California (where their Grandmother was in hospice). The next morning I confronted him with the emails and tried calmly to tell him to pack his bags and GET OUT. He was explosive and angry, but never admitted anything. He grabbed some old towels and cut them into small pieces to put them in a gym bag. As he continued screaming and acting out of control – which was nothing new in our house – I got in my car (making sure my boys were not home for the night).

He was explosive. While I was in the car as he called my cell incessantly. I finally answered and told him to GET OUT, and when I get back from California, we will talk. He was more concerned about the dinner plans we had with neighbors than what was really happening with our marriage. He was in absolute denial and had zero emotional connect. As usual I gave in. After meeting out neighbors for dinner (business as usual for him... laughing and joking), he checked into a motel.

I was in absolute shock to experience his unwillingness to make no attempt to make amends or discuss a solution. I wanted to discuss and get to the truth. He acted as if he had no idea why I kicked him out and did not seem to care.

The next day, in the pouring rain, he begged to meet me at a deli in the middle of town. When he showed up, he could not look me in the eye and had nothing to say. He was so brazen to sit across the table after sharing twenty years of marriage and not be willing to discuss why he now had a male lover. His only concern was, "Where do you expect me to stay?" No mention of our boys. Our marriage was soon to end, and he was worried about saving face and looking good in town. He had no concern about his children or the lives he had damaged behind.

After returning from California (no attempts made to discuss anything on his part) I managed to force the GEX to meet again with a marriage counselor. He reluctantly showed up late to the appointment. He was disheveled, ornery, and belligerent. It was at this time that I read thru my notes and told him to finally come clean. I was trying to make it a business deal; otherwise, I would emotionally fold and I felt that he would love to see me crumble in pain. He started talking in circles just like a politician that he was.

He was acting more fierce and forceful. He was actually making me nervous. I finally took out my phone and read his sexting text. He froze and tried to grab my phone to delete it. The counselor stopped him and said, "What does this mean?" GEX tried to explain "It was nothing. I was just texting a guy from Equinox Gym. I said, "If that is nothing then what is really going on?" That's when the flood gates opened. He said, "It started years ago with an incident at the gym in the sauna. One thing lead to another. It has been years of whatever and now I have a young lover for the past two plus years. He said it so matter of fact and calmly. He showed no remorse or concern. He actually had a bravado relieved look on his face. I was in a complete state of shock and did not know whether to cry, scream, or punch him. It was all out in the open finally only because I was one of the lucky abused women to find out the truth on my own. The coward would have preferred not to tell me. He admitted that he wanted to continue to live a double life and hoped that eventually we would be so emotionally and physically disconnected that I would walk out on him!

My GEX was a divorce and criminal defense attorney in addition to being our elected local judge. The entire community knew our family. I was fighting an uphill battle in a no-fault court system. I would have to thoroughly prepare myself and "fasten my seat belt" and try to get a lawyer who would protect my best interest.

My first court date was a nightmare. The judge (who knew my EX) almost mocked me by saying, "Your husband could have sex with a monkey and will not put money in your pocket!" I was never going to get anywhere in the court system and would have to find a way to get rid of lawyers and settle quickly.

The next few months were horrible trying to sell our house and get my son into college while paying unnecessary legal fees. He was hiding all his assets and I was depleting my resources. I refused to talk to him because all he did was yell and act like a lunatic. He had no sense of guilt or remorse. He had moved on in life with his gay young Asian lover that he was cheating with for over 2 years!

I did not interpret any warning signs correctly. The last three years of our marriage were very disturbing to me and my children. There was a complete disconnect and lack of any family values. If he was not at the gym working out, he was hiding in the basement or behind a Netflix Show or looking at porn on his iPad (now I know that.) He was completely argumentative and belligerent. Everything was my fault. My boys could no longer handle the constant fighting and opted to stay away from our home and hang out with friends whenever possible. Something as simple as taking our dog for a walk in the meadow or attending a concert and dancing in the aisle was taboo. I felt like I was walking on eggshells and so emotionally constrained and actually fearful from his inexplicable outbursts of anger. Yes, there were signs and evidence of some enhancement pills and body building powders. Also he was looking in the mirror and spending more and more time at the gym while leaving the house for no apparent reason.

Our lives revolved around his image and the upcoming election. It was all about HIM and putting on a show. Everything was turning into a façade and all of a sudden my GEX wanted to travel and spend money that we should have been saving for college tuition. Nothing made any sense to me.

I was trying to work on my kids and keep our family intact, and he wanted to be the center of attention every minute of the day... Remember he was the judge (finally won the election at the emotional and financial expense of his family). He was the Sunday lector in our Roman Catholic Church. He would lector every Sunday. This upstanding church goer was actively cheating on his wife and children with men for years.

He never would have admitted anything to me because he was a true coward. I think these men are obviously struggling from low esteem. They are trying to identify with the proper gender and cannot identify easily when under pressure. I think they harbor such anger and resentment. That is why they hide behind their family and their politics and religion to disguise who they really are. It is such a sad display of humanity and their lives are really a lie and a misconception. He struggled with his sexuality his whole life took him two wives and two children to come out of the closet at 60 years of age.

Gay issue aside, why handle the matter in such a selfish deceptive manner? There is nothing wrong with being gay, but the façade and deception and cheating is the issue. On top of it, he did not admit to the deception and do the right thing financially for your family. The GEX knew the "no fault" divorce system and the courts would work in his favor. He was prepared. These men are selfish cowards. Yet they get all the support they need thru meet up groups and media and the court protects them financially. They have the support groups and Meet-up groups. They act like the poor victim who had to hide their true identity due to our cruel society.

The saddest part in my opinion is the lack of remorse and the ability for these gay men to move on so quickly with their lovers and their new lives at the expense of their families. All of a sudden they can travel the world and spend money and do things that they never had the emotional or financial ability to do with their children and wives.

I actually received a strange type written letter in my mail box before I served him divorce papers. The letter was so lame and poorly written. The gist was so cruel and psychopathic. My GEX wanted me to know that if he had to do it again he would! He was getting close to 60 years old and he had to "prove his masculinity ". That sounds like an oxymoron. He had to prove he was gay to be a man? What does that mean? He also said he was purposely creating distance and dissension knowing it would destroy everything. He said, "I did it willingly and with my eyes wide open. I gave into my weakness 2.5 years ago and there is NO turning back." I was trapped and holding you hostage. I resented you every day for trying to make me straight and narrow. This letter goes on with the same tone. I would call this a far cry from an apology.

In conclusion being gay is not the issue. The main concern is why these men decided to marry in the first place (my GEX was married once before with a child). They have children and families and pretend to be fathers and husbands to hide their true identity. They are selfish cowards who act like they are victims when the truth comes out. They actually are allowed to receive the Sacrament of Marriage to cover up and then when the truth unravels they go to Confession and brag about their sinful acts. These men have no moral compass. It is all about them and their needs at any given moment. Did they not stand on the altar and speak the vows, "For rich and poor until death do we part?"

Divorce is extremely difficult to accept on every level. Emotionally, financially, and the children suffer the most. These evil men knew from the time they were youngsters that something was different. Not to be harsh but they should have come to terms and opened up before things got out of control and they could no longer suppress their true sexual identity. I actually admire the young men who figure out they are gay in their teens. They are brave young men who have not destroyed families as a result of acting on impulse and lying and cheating behind the backs of their wives and children. The pretense and charade over twenty years of marriage is the hardest part to digest. How could this man even try to fulfill a role of father and husband when the majority of their lives were a lie? With that said, my best advice is no contact at all if possible. The GEX has moved on years ago and trust me he wants no reminder of the family he so dramatically left behind.

Cindy's Story: "Onward"

I divorced the man I love. Who does that after *43 years* of a happy, "best friends" marriage?

The answer: *A woman who discovers her husband is gay.*

I was 20 years old when I married my high school sweetheart in 1974, and I was always happy. We never argued, never had a cross word, and we raised three children. He was my "best friend." I trusted him, I believed him, and I knew he loved me. I always put my husband first and my children. He took care of me when I was sick. He was a good father. He was kind, he was gentle, he was giving, and I felt protected and loved.

We made a great team. Until, November 2017, my world changed instantly. My husband went into the hospital for a minor heart procedure. His anesthesiologist entered the pre-operation room and questioned my husband how he contracted hepatitis B. My husband was partially sedated and didn't respond to his question.

I answered the anesthesiologist that his records were incorrect that my husband was diagnosed years ago with hepatitis A due to contaminated seafood, not hepatitis B. The anesthesiologist insisted his medical records were correct and left the room. As my husband was transferred to the operating room, my memory flashed back to the gay porn magazines I had discovered 13 years earlier. I had confronted my husband 13 years ago after I discovered gay porn magazines. He dismissed them as a joke someone was playing on him, and I believed him. I know how hepatitis B is contracted--it spreads through contact with blood, semen or other bodily fluids. Having unprotected sex, especially with homosexual males, puts one at high risk.

The first thing all women must do when they suspect their husband of being gay or even having knowledge he had a sexual encounter with another is to get tested. Do not believe anything they may tell you, just protect yourself, get tested. Even though I had not had sexual intercourse with my husband for the last 12 years of my marriage, I immediately went to my doctor, told him of my suspicions about my husband, and was tested for STDs, AIDS, and Hepatitis. After a long 72 hours, my test results were negative.

My husband recovered from his heart procedure, and for three months following his procedure, I went home with him, and never confronted him regarding my suspicions; instead, I played detective. The more I searched the worse it got. I discovered gay porn magazines, gay porn sites, and dildos. I discovered Internet searches for gay bars, for gay escort services, and for adult bookstores. I searched his map quest, and discovered locations where he traveled such as strip clubs and gay bars. I discovered a gay dating site, where he developed a profile looking for a male, "to have discreet sexual relations." One of my worst discoveries was fecal splatter on the outside of his pants.

Finally, the day of confrontation came, and I had enough evidence. As we sat in our new retirement home in Florida, I calmly asked my husband, "I know your secret, how many men have you slept with?" A look of fear came across his face, but not one word of the truth did he speak. He denied, denied and denied. Over the weeks, his stories were consistently changing as my head was spinning. I was trying to make sense of his nonsense. I wanted so badly to believe him; I tried to convince myself his explanations and excuses were truthful. His first excuse, he contracted hepatitis B from being drunk and having anal sex with a woman. His second excuse, he was raped by three men. His explanations/excuses always included the statement, "I am not gay." Eventually, his statements changed from, "I am bi-curious," to, "I am bisexual," to, "It only happened one time." I just wanted the truth--I wanted validation. So I devised a plan. I called my husband when I was on a business trip and led him to believe we could work out a plan to satisfy his sexual needs and asked him what he would need for sexual satisfaction. He responded, "I want to have sex with a businessman once a month," and, "a young guy would be a turn on." That was the worst day of my life--*those words crushed me*. I realized I can't fix this, my marriage is over. I filed for divorce.

Red Flags:

So were there red flags? I read somewhere that there were never any red flags but maybe very subtle red flags or slightly pink flags. It is hard to say there were warning signs because they were not loud enough or bright enough to heed a warning. There were plenty of "Pink Flags," but the Red Flags not so much until later, 42 years later.

The slightly "Pink Flags":

He was never romantic; he never kissed my head or caressed my hair or patted my bottom, or held me, really held me close. No passionate kisses, just "Grandma like" kisses on my cheek. I never felt like he made love to me, I felt like he "serviced me;" our sexual encounters were brief, one step, two step, done. Frequency of sex was limited; we never made love in a hotel room or when we were on vacations.

He was homophobic. He would make inappropriate gay jokes. He was so insecure. He was always worried about his image and what other people thought of him. He was obsessed about his body and how he looked. He would comment on how other males looked, but never females He never noticed attractive females as they walked by, I mistakenly took this as a compliment towards me, showing me respect. He only showed me affection in public, when we were around other couples, or his business associates, then he would hold my hand and kiss my cheek. I now know he was putting on a performance for those around him. He was playing the role of a straight man/husband.

He lied. He lied about where he was, or even minor things. I excused his lying believing he had a bad memory.

I felt more like "His buddy," or "best friend," than his wife or lover. I felt more that he needed me, than loved me. I was never number one in his life, his needs always came first. He would never walk beside me, always walked ahead of me.

The Red Flags:

The major red flag: he never desired me as a woman. I can see this now. I was so young, 20 years old when I got married, I knew no differently and I loved him.

I didn't understand the red flags until it was too late. Even when I discovered gay porn magazines at age 50, I accepted his response that it was just a joke. I asked him if he was gay, after this discovery of gay porn and he screamed at me, "I am not gay." That's what I wanted to believe, I choose to believe him, but, maybe then I knew on some level and I was afraid of the truth, so I let it be. I realize now, maybe I went into denial then, perhaps I subconsciously went into that closet with him, I blocked it out cause I loved him.

At the age of 50, my husband claimed he had erectile dysfunction, and blamed me for his inability to have an erection during our limited sexual encounters. He claimed his ED was the result of me having a hysterectomy. So at age 50, my limited sex life ended completely. Truth is, I also lost any desire for him sexually, because it just did not seem genuine, he was like a robot. Why did I accept this? Because I loved him.

Over time, at 43 years later, my discovery of gay porn, dildos, naked pictures of my husband on his cell phone, hepatitis B diagnosis and google searches on his cell phone for gay bars, gay escort services, gay sensual massages, gay dating sites are more than just red flags, that is just hard core evidence: He's Gay. I can't block this out, I have to step out of that closet, face my reality. Onward.

I have realized that I was used, and perhaps some would say I was a "beard." He cast me in a role of his wife, and I was his cover. Only in public showing me affection, holding my hand, kissing my cheek, only when there was an audience. He played his role well, a straight man, a straight husband, he was a performer. I refuse to wear that label of "beard," I was not a willing participate in his play. Cast me out, curtain closed. Onward.

For months, following my discovery of "the gay thing," (TGT) I had overwhelming sadness. I wanted my happiness back. I have never known such emotional pain, the one person who I trusted most in this world, who I knew would always be there for me, was not the man I thought he was. I felt so used, he has no right to do this to me. I was not valued, I was not respected, and I was not loved. His parting words to me were, "No one will ever love you like I love you." Now that is one statement I know is true, I will never be "loved" like that again. I struggle at times, now with, what is love? I truly loved my husband, now ex-husband, but I have come to the realization that, I loved the man he pretended to be, not who he actually is. There are times, when I am so fragile, the overwhelming sadness creeps in, all my memories are tainted with lies. But facing the truth I was used for 43 years, a lifetime, is my most difficult challenge. My second difficult challenge, "What is love?" Onward.

I feel so cheated, so used, so betrayed. I just want to be loved. I would always tell my children, "It's good to be loved." And this man, who I loved for 43 years, has never apologized, he has never been able to assume any responsibility for this betrayal for this fraud. He believes he was, quote, "a good husband." There comes a point in this healing journey where there is acceptance. Once I gave myself that gift of acceptance, I was able to move forward. The moment I accepted that my husband was gay, and I could not "fix this," I started to focus on me. It was no longer about him. I made a conscious choice, not to go down that rabbit hole of being bitter or angry. I was 63 years old, and what time I have left on this earth, I want to be happy. I knew exactly what I wanted, I want truth, honesty, integrity and happiness in my life. And if that meant being alone, so be it. Onward.

I had those dark depression days, I couldn't get out of bed. I would look back on my life and try to figure it out, what was real, what was not, finally I came to the conclusion, it was my life and it was real for me. I led it with dignity and truth. I was a good person, I was kind to others, and I loved with all my heart. So I pushed forward, I have to, it's the only way I can survive. Onward.

I could never have gotten through this journey without my trusted friends, they were my lifeline. Professional therapy was beneficial to a point, it put things in perspective for me very quickly. But I just got tired, very tired of talking about what my husband did to me, his betrayal and his lies. He took enough years of my life, and I just didn't want to give him anymore of my precious time. I am done with him, completely done. So what, if he will never assume any responsibility for his actions or apologize for his betrayal and all the pain he cause me. It is no longer about him. I have choices and I am going to make the best life for myself. Onward.

I am blessed with three children out of this, "marriage." So I have no regrets. Without this "marriage," I would not have them nor my three grandchildren. Well, maybe I have a few regrets. One of the mistakes, I made in this process, is initially using my daughters as a "support system." **Warning: Don't use your children as your support system**. Bonnie Kaye has warned us about this. I shared some details about their father I should not have shared, Big Mistake. Even though, I have apologized, my oldest daughter has not forgiven me, it has destroyed our relationship. And sadly, she has placed conditions where and when I can see the grandchildren. Thankfully, my youngest daughter and son are supportive and show kindness and love towards me. My children have been able to maintain a close, loving relationship with their father. I maintain an amicable relationship with my ex-gay-husband, for the sake of my children and grandchildren. In some strange way, I still care about him, but I also dislike him, I strongly dislike him, I have no respect left for him. I see now who he actually is, he is manipulative, he is selfish, he is narcissistic, he is a coward, and he is a gay man, who made a conscious choice to use me, to protect his false self, his false image. Onward.

And so I buried him. My straight husband was dead, he was gone forever, and he was never coming back. My life was never going to be the same. I felt like a widow, I grieved, I cried, and for the first time in 43 years, I was alone. I no longer had, "my best friend," I no longer had, "my loyal, devoted husband." Fear ruled me. Who would love me? Who would take care of me when I was sick? My biggest fear, I didn't want to die alone. His funeral services were private, only a few of my close trusted friends were invited. These friends were my support system, my therapy, my safety net. They knew every detail of his passing, they allowed me to share my grief, they listened to me, they held me, and they loved me. After the funeral, my pronoun usage changed from, "we" to "I." Onward.

For the first time in 43 years, it is all about me. I realize I am responsible for myself and I am responsible for my own happiness. I choose happiness over bitterness and anger. There are still times, where I am coexisting between sadness and happiness. There are times, when I am so fragile, the overwhelming sadness visits, but not for long. I finally got out of bed and I got busy, busy with my new life. I traveled, joined book clubs, volunteered at church, joined club activities, learned to play pickle ball and mahjong, fostered new friendships, and established a close network of friends. Onward

I push through the sadness, by distraction, and by making the choice to move forward. Some days I am okay; some days I am not. But I never remain still. I refuse to stay in limbo. I refuse to be paralyzed by fear. I push forward. I do my best not to live in the past, and focus on the wrongs that have been done to me. I don't want to be a victim. So I make a choice to live in the present and focus on the future. I hold onto that gift of acceptance. With that gift of acceptance, there is no more struggle, no more tears, no fear, there is just peace. Onward.

I still have difficulties setting boundaries with my ex-gay-husband. He wants to be "friends," he still calls me for advice and we talk about the children and grandchildren. I feel pity for him, he is a tortured soul, who doesn't want to be gay. With time he will find another "beard," it's just a matter of time. I could honestly be happy for him, if he could lead his authentic life, and find a loving relationship with man, instead of choosing to deceive another woman. But he remains in denial and continues to engage in secret gay activities. But it is no longer about him, it is about me. Onward.

The first year after the divorce, I finally got comfortable being alone at the age of 64 years old, and I was happy. I established a fulfilling life, busy with travel, volunteering, and social activities. And then I met someone. He is a man of integrity, he is a true gentleman. And he desires me as a woman. I never knew romance before. The subtle ways he shows me he cares, the kiss on my forehead, the kiss on the back of my hand, caressing my face, or the pat on my bottom. Opening car doors for me, holding my hand, cuddling and spooning. Cooking meals for me, bringing me flowers. He shows me through his actions not his words that he cares for me. But, the problem is with me, not him. I trust him. But I don't trust myself, I think I love him, but "What is love?" I am afraid my heart will be broken. I was OK being alone, I could manage that but loving someone, I am so afraid. So for now, I do my best not to analyze the relationship, just enjoying spending time with him, and holding onto the belief, that no matter what happens, I will be okay. I got my happiness back, and I am okay. Onward.

Angela's Story

I was married to my gay husband (GH) for 15 years and dated him for 18 months before marrying him. At the time of writing, our divorce has been final three years. My relationship with my gay husband began when a mutual friend set us up on a date. I had gone to college with him, and knew of him, but had never spoken to him. He had a large group of male friends from college, and some were also his life-long friends, which gave him credibility. He had a reputation for being fun and a good person. I remember myself as being vibrant and happy, with many good friends, working hard, and making my way career wise.

He held me captive with surreal experiences of romance and expectation during the courtship period, with elegant dinners and compliments. He guided me to look to the future, eluding that it would be more of the same but even better. The experiences together were rich with good times and what felt like an authentic connection. During the courtship phase, we would recall each date and reminisce about each one and relive them.

I learned he had never had a girlfriend during this time, but he said he had had sex with a few women I knew, but ended things with them because they were shallow. There was something about him that seemed innocent, almost righteous, which made him seem trustworthy. He listened during our conversations and made time for me. He didn't pressure me to have sex with him ever, which I appreciated as a Christian woman wanting to wait this time.

His charm, mixed with a sense of self-deprecating humor, always made me laugh before we married. I perceived him to be humble and have integrity because he seemed aware of his less than perfectness, which made him seem perfect in an ironic way. Early on, he shared that his father emotionally abused him. The stories were heartbreaking, and I felt sorry for him, and bonded me to him since he trusted me enough to share. Later, his stories of abuse also set me up to be suspicious of his family's treatment of him, and not question the troubled family dynamics of which my husband was responsible.

While we were dating, he pretended not to have any money to test if I genuinely loved him. We never discussed finances even after we got married. He told me we were fine, and I didn't need to worry about that. He insisted I quit my job, which left me with no income. I think I accepted this because I had grown up poor, and my career was in an industry that was very competitive and low paying. I had more security in my marriage financially than ever before in my life. The security came at a cost, though, as I always felt terrible and guilty for spending money because he would belittle me when I did. To cope, I tried not to spend as best I could. He refused to sit down with me and discuss a budget. Not having a budget kept me stuck and always susceptible to his anger and disappointment. During the last few years of our marriage, I discovered that he had put money in bank account in only his name without telling me. I feared he had been hiding money from me.

The wedding ceremony and reception foreshadowed my marriage. I wish I would have stayed with how terrible that night made me feel and had taken action to dissolve the marriage immediately. During the church ceremony, while we were at the altar and about to exchange our vows, the room was silent, and my GH dropped my wedding ring! There was a sudden chime of my delicate gold wedding ring hitting the tile floor. Everyone laughed, and my GH loved the attention. He made a funny face back to the crowd of over 200 people who roared even louder. Before the ceremony, the priest told my gay husband that whatever happens, do not leave your bride at the altar, even if you drop the ring! Sadly, at the moment that was supposed to be full of sacred promises, he left me standing alone at the altar, and he got down on his hands and knees to look for the ring. The whole ordeal foreshadowed his dropping his commitment to me, and me being alone. Surely when some of the guests- my GH's friends and family laughed, they undoubtedly knew my GH's secret and were also laughing at me for marrying a gay man. Shortly after the wedding, he lost his wedding ring and refused to replace it or ever wear one.

At the wedding reception, I couldn't find my GH. Unbeknownst to me, he had left the wedding with a male "friend" and went to a bar for a couple of hours and got drunk. When he returned, he lied and told me he was talking with his parent's friends. "Right over there." I was at my wedding alone. His father told me the truth that my gay husband had left the reception. I met with my gay husband's father after seeking help when my GH refused to engage in the divorce process. I had been waiting for a year and a half for him to respond to documents served. It was the first honest conversation I had with anyone in his family. But the weight of learning that my GH left our wedding crushed me. And, it devastated me that his father and others knew my GH was gay, but stood by and did nothing. They just watched as me and my children suffer for all those years.

On our wedding night, my GH said he was too tired to make love. He used the same excuse on our honeymoon, also, and throughout our marriage. Other reasons to not have sex, or even hug or touch me were: he felt too sick, he had terrible allergies, or he was too hungover. When he felt okay, he would criticize me and complain to trigger me and anger me so I wouldn't want to be with him.

After we said our vows, it was like a new person took over my husband's body. The man I dated wasn't there anymore. I believed he was still in there somewhere and that what we had was real and could still be if I could be good enough and make him love me again. So I worked hard for 15 years to fix myself, fix my husband, and fix our children. I tried to be perfect in every way, and I created a warm, loving home. I tried to get him to be home more and spend time with the kids and me. But nothing worked, and I felt so alone, totally rejected, and hopeless. I lost my sense of self and accepted 100% of our problems were my fault because I was damaged, flawed, and innately bad. I wanted to die.

My gay husband spent most of his time away from us working, entertaining clients, and openly traveling with male friends who shared a passion for a particular sport, two to three weeks out of every month. Once, he went on a long trip with "friends" and came home with a severe staphylococcal infection in his anus that spread down his entire thigh and required intravenous treatments at the hospital. He said he fell, and the injury got infected.

I didn't suspect that he was gay. It never crossed my mind because I did not know that gay men married straight women. And my GH was consistent in how he described what he was doing and where he was going. He consistently went on trips with a specific group of friends from college, which I now know is a group of single gay men, and gay men married to women or divorced. He was either with them, out with other men, or working. He spoke in code. When he had a "meeting," he was going on a lunch date with a man, and "out with friends" meant meeting a man for drinks at night. I think his consistent use of language helped his behavior seem normal, and I accepted what he said because it didn't seem out of the ordinary. He would send giant flower arrangements whenever he would travel or have "meetings" where he got home late. I finally saw the pattern but thought he was cheating on me with other women. He would flirt inappropriately with every female, the mortgage brokers, real estate agents, friends, waitresses, retail clerks, teachers, and counselors to make me and everyone think he was straight.

I always felt disconnected from him. I wanted more intimacy, more time, and more attention. He told me I was selfish, not giving enough, expected too much, and he always found something wrong with me. After we had our third baby, he told me he wasn't attracted to me anymore and that he sees me as a mother and "just can't do that with you anymore." We rarely had sex before the final rejection. Sex only happened if he was utterly drunk after a party. Sex with him was robotic and ended quickly. There was no passion, and he wouldn't look at me, kiss me, or touch me. He often had scabs on his penis that he couldn't explain. And he kept several bottles of a product called new skin liquid bandage everywhere; in his car, the bathroom, and his luggage. By the end of our marriage, he said he was impotent. I believed that he hated me and was disgusted by me. He said our marriage caused him to feel depressed and anxious. He used to hit and kick me while I slept and tell me laughing, he was dreaming and unaware.

I coped by crying in the shower so my kids wouldn't see or hear me, and I slept on the couch on and off. I prayed constantly.

We somehow managed to have three kids over 15 years. It seems like he just went along with creating a family to keep up appearances and hide his gayness. I think it made him feel more masculine to be a father. Even though he didn't bond with the kids, he capitalized on the father-child events, such as leading father-daughter groups that went on camping trips and co-coaching many of my son's sports teams. My gay husband was adamant about being the one to take my son to his practices, even if he wasn't the coach. I think he was having sex with one of the other father coaches. One coach would continuously call my gay husband, and he would laugh and say the coach was butt dialing him. I believe he was calling my GH to hook up.

My gay husband told me his family hated me and thought I was a terrible mother. He told them I disliked them too, and that I didn't want them to come over to our house. Because of this, I dreaded seeing his family, and I felt so uncomfortable around them. Still, I hosted holiday events to make them like me. I was filled with anxiety and sadness because I genuinely gave them all that was in me through my cooking, gifts, and preparing my home. My GH would tell me his family disapproved of my efforts and said I acted awkward and uncomfortable. Whenever I stood up to my GH or questioned him, he would threaten to take my children, home, and money, and leave me with nothing. He said because his family hated me too, they would help him destroy me.

In the morning or whenever he entered a room, he would say hello and address everyone but me. He ignored me and acted like I wasn't there. It was so awful to be invisible to him because I couldn't figure out what I had done to deserve the treatment, and I couldn't solve the problem of him having disdain for me.

Unexplainable things happened during this time. Money in my wallet would be missing. My GH would blame the housekeeper/ babysitter, and so I accused her and fired her, leaving me with no help. Other things disappeared too. I think my GH was taking these things to make me feel unsafe in my home, and he egged the fear on and seemed to enjoy my discomfort. Sometimes when he would walk away, I would catch a sinister smile on his face.

Several strange men came to our house looking for my GH and asked for him by name when he wasn't home. After one of his "meetings," my GH brought home a male enhancement/ aphrodisiac product he said was given to him by the friend he had a "meeting." He put it in our refrigerator where the children could see it. When questioned about it, he acted like it was normal to come home with it, even though he hadn't attempted to have sex with me for years.

My GH got a text from an older gentleman that said: "I'm thinking about you; please call me." His phone records showed him to be on the phone for hours with several different men in different cities and states. His travel receipts showed he traveled to other places than he said he was traveling. He lied about where he was and then would forget what he said and change his story when questioned or deny and lie his way out of it, even if the children caught him and asked him about it. It was like a game to him.

The places that we frequented, my children's' tutoring center, a facility near our home, the office building where my GH business mentor worked, the food court my husband frequented, were all listed on a gay site as places to hook up with gay men in the bathrooms in our town. I Googled "where to hook up with gay men."

One time my GH offered to take the kids to dinner, I joined them at the last minute. I could tell he was disappointed. There we ran into a stranger, a man with a cute dog. Later I figured out that my GH was in a relationship with this man, and my GH had set up this "chance" meeting so his "friend" could meet my children.

We went to church regularly, and I often noticed a man I went to high school with always alone in the back of the church - behind wherever we were seated. It was a subtle presence, but I got the sense he was waiting for us. Sometimes my husband would cry in church and leave to go to the bathroom. The man would go to the bathroom at the same time. They became close friends, always getting together for drinks and spending time together, mostly when the man's wife was out of town. Yes, the man is married with children.

My GH pursued a few other married men I had gone to high school with, inviting them over to our home for dinner and drinks when their wives were out of town, and meeting up with them when he traveled because they "coincidently happened to be there too."

I insisted we go to therapy (for most years) and attend a church group for healing relationships. Without fail, each therapist we saw determined I was the one with the problem and needed extra therapy sessions, which I faithfully attended. I sought help from the church group, but the leader insisted I could not divorce my husband because he had done nothing wrong. Now I know that I was psychologically abused and had every reason to leave him.

Even though I felt stuck and frustrated, I got emotionally and physically healthier and got into physical shape. However, my husband still wasn't kind to me and still had no interest in me. I was determined to win him over, and I got plastic surgery (a mommy makeover). I thought he would be attracted to the new and improved me, but he wasn't. Friends and family told me I looked beautiful and this support made me think that maybe the problem wasn't me. I became distraught and went to a new therapist alone. She advised he showed signs of being a narcissist. As per my therapist's advice, I asked my GH to separate, which he gladly agreed. We rented a second home and took turns nesting with our children in our primary residence; each stayed at a rental house while the other spent time with the kids in the family house. Nesting didn't work out because my GH brought men to the rental home or would lie and say he was staying there when he was really somewhere else.

I had been praying for years for wisdom about my marriage; to know what the problem was. At the end of the marriage, I broke down one day, unable to get out of bed. I cried and pleaded with God to give me wisdom about what was wrong with my marriage and why my husband didn't love me. I suddenly heard a clear inner voice whisper, "he's gay." It felt like a miracle to have this inner knowing. It all made sense now, and I felt great relief and had clarity. I felt deep compassion for my husband, and I felt shame and regret, cruel for not knowing sooner.

I went to him and asked him if he is gay. In the same breath, I apologized for not knowing sooner. I offered to allow him to tell our children and bring his partner into our family, not realizing there were multiple partners! As I spoke, his face softened, his shoulders dropped, and I could see his body melt and relax. Someone new stepped forward in his body. His eyes lit up and glowed a little, and I sensed his heartwarming as he received what I said. I could tell he felt loved and seen in a new way! He expressed that he has never felt so accepted in his entire life. And just as I thought we were having the most brilliant and significant breakthrough of our lives, he stood straight up and pivoted, his face full of agony, he said in a panic, "if this gets out, I will be ruined!" And with that, he looked at me with a blank stare and, declared, "I'm not gay," and walked out of the room. I sat alone on the bed, confused and dumbfounded.

From that moment on, he used gaslighting and intimidation to protect his secret, never confessed or apologized for misrepresenting himself, or using me, and emotionally abusing my children and me. His behavior outside the marriage of meeting up with men became more frequent and more brazen, while at the same time, he vowed to want the marriage to work.

To convince me, he went to a Christian men's retreat to recommit himself to God and wore a bracelet as a symbol of being a "man of Jesus" for about a week. He said he went to therapy every week and was making progress. He said he did not have sex with me because he masturbated in the shower, which didn't make sense or seem like a logical excuse to me.

During the year after hearing the voice telling me my GH is gay, I felt unsafe around him. We remained married but separated because I so desperately wanted to believe that he was heterosexual, and I needed proof that he was gay before I could leave him. The decision was paramount. By the end of that difficult year, I decided to pretend things were getting better for me in the marriage so he would feel more secure in his secret. Sure enough, he lied about where he was spending time and with whom. I planted a cell phone in his car and used GPS to document his whereabouts. I hired a private investigator to follow him, who confirmed my GH was out with men and was lying to me.

Unfortunately, during this time, someone slashed my tires on three different occasions. They cut my tire with a knife and put a nail in sideways so the tire would pop when I drove. Someone drained the brake fluid from my car, and someone scratched every square inch of my car with a key. Money was wired mysteriously out of our checking account from GH's computer, and he refused to report it to the police. He had a panic attack when I told him I would report it, and he started crying, begging me not to tell the police he is gay. I was shocked that he said that and thought him being gay had nothing to do with the money missing, but quickly realized that someone he had brought home most likely stole the money. There was also an international charge on my credit card the same day for a book called "coming out" that he insists he didn't purchase. I received text messages from gay men looking for men and drug dealers selling drugs in the middle of the night for a few years. It was as if my GH was giving out my number as a joke. I changed my phone number seven times. Finally, I got a new phone number and only gave it to my GH. Sure enough, the harassing calls and texts continued. I had proof he was harassing me. I told the police, but they said they could not help me.

I began to fear for my life and still do today. I don't know who my GH is or what he is capable of doing. I know he hates me and feels threatened by me. I fear he will have me killed one day after I raise our children, to prevent me from telling anyone he is gay.

I filled for divorce and decided I needed to move a few hours away from my hometown to get to safety. I changed the locks on my house and put my GH's things in the garage for him to pick up. I found bizarre hidden storage shelves high up in the garage that he had built to store items, but they were empty by then.

I started investigating the people my GH had traveled with and especially the men my GH took pictures of with our family camera on a recent trip with "Christian men." Yes, he used our family camera on a trip. A gay male dating website featured one of the men pictured in my camera. It showed that he lived in our town and was in the same industry as my GH. It only took one search.

Eventually, my children and I moved a few hours away from my GH, but he followed us and moved too. Unfortunately, he got into a relationship with a married man at my children's school in our new town. One of the married men's daughters confronted my child in front of other kids at school, saying, "Why is your dad always at my house? What he is doing is wrong, and your dad is a creep." Her friends berated my child too and my child was humiliated and refused to return to school.

My child went to therapy, and my GH started to interfere with the treatment by seeing the same therapist. GH and my child tried to work out and move beyond what happened at the school, but my GH would only talk about how he's not gay. GH insisted my child agree that he wasn't gay. My child stated that it didn't matter to him if GH is gay; he loves and accepts him no matter what. That wasn't enough for my GH, and my GH got angry and upset.

He filed a lawsuit against me for parental alienation and accused me of telling my kids he is gay. He asked the court to order my children and me to attend reunification therapy with him. My child had already spent months in therapy with my GH, and our other children don't know he is gay, and they freely visited him whenever he wants to see them. The lawsuit was unfounded. I had to attend therapy with my ex-GH for six months. My child had to give his account of the events at school with the children. I reported how my youngest child was often left unsafely outside public restrooms while my GH was inside. And, how my GH insisted on taking my children camping to a man's house every time they visited, and my children refused to go. In the end, the therapist determined I had not alienated my children. My ex-GH dropped the lawsuit after I told him everything he had filed thus far, is now on the public record. He didn't know that and didn't like that!

Now my ex-GH sees the children once every few weeks for dinner only, whenever he feels like it. He dropped the visiting schedule of every other weekend immediately after the therapy ended. He seems to have settled into his life of partying and traveling. He does whatever he wants, whenever he wants, the same as when we were married. Nothing has changed. I'm still raising the kids alone, but thankfully I am free from his abuse and lies. The kids suspect he put spyware on their phones and computers. He knows when they are online, what is in their texts, and when they are not at home. We've had to replace phones and computers to stop the spying.

I am learning to trust myself and my perceptions again. I don't have much confidence and feel so ashamed about what happened to me. I know my ex-GH tells anyone and everyone negative things about me: teachers, counselors, children's friends' parents, his family, and tries to triangulate me in relationships. Children's' school events are excruciating. He shows up happy and tan and acts as the life of the party chatting with the fathers. I have gained weight from stress eating and sadness, and I am embarrassed about how my looks have deteriorated. I want to crawl in a hole at these public events that feel like a slap in the face. I don't say negative things about him or defend myself because I fear what he will do to me, and because two of my children don't know he is gay. It seems best to focus on the future and not engage with other about him.

It is a battle to move forward, but there is no going back. It is so painful not to be able to share my truth with old and new friends. And it makes me feel crazy, not knowing who I can trust. Which friends' husbands have my ex-GH been with in the past, or is with right now? And, it's hard for my friends and family to understand my experience or the magnitude of the self-healing I am undertaking when I can't share with them the truth about my marriage and the psychological abuse I endured. I left the town I grew up in and most of my life-long friends. I didn't keep in touch with most of them. I assume they believe the negative things he says about me to their husbands which is devastating.

I'm repairing my sense of self, while at the same time raising kids (who are struggling with the divorce, leaving our home, schools, friends, and are nervous that our finances have changed for the worse). I am focused on keeping a comfortable and safe home, educating myself, developing skills, and building up my self-esteem to step out into the world more and open a business. I don't feel comfortable to date. So much of my energy goes to managing the fear I have of my ex. It is like a subtle vibration that runs through my bones and is always running in the background. If I sit still and get present, sometimes my body shakes. It reminds me of my past and sometimes paralyzes me, while other times it empowers me to keep moving forward to mend myself and reclaim my life no matter what. I know I can do it because I have already come so far.

The story you are about to read is from a straight sister in Pakistan, a culture far more restrictive and less understanding than ours in America.

S's Story – River of Fire

That day of April, 2014, is the day when everything in my life came crashing down, destroying my life along with any semblance or sanity which it had, or rather I thought it had, in its aftermath. If I had died that day, the story of my life would have ended in a tragedy. I would have gone to my grave as a victim, a woman who never had the courage or self-respect to stand up for herself. But God was kind to me. He made me live. He made me walk through that unimaginable river of fire, and with His help, I was able to emerge on the other side--badly scorched, burnt, and broken--but alive and with a desire to live and heal. I consider myself fortunate that now I will go to my grave as a survivor, dignified and respected by those who matter.

I belong to an enlightened but traditional family. In our country, 'good girls' kept away from boys and always agreed to arranged marriages. I wanted to be a good girl, so I agreed to whomever my parents chose for me. Amongst the scores of proposals, my parents chose the one they thought was the best match. We met at a relative's house, and I liked him. His parents wanted an engagement ceremony so I assumed he also liked me. We talked on the phone a few times during our six-month engagement. Twice he also came over with his younger brother. Then we got married.

I didn't experience feelings of love or happiness even in our early days. He seemed withdrawn and unhappy to me. Whenever I tried to come close or show affection, he would discourage me. Unlike other newlyweds, he never wanted to spend time with me; on the contrary he was always looking forward to be on his own. Our sex life was also very confusing for me. Since I had no prior experience with boys, emotionally or physically, there were many things which were not clear to me. Initial days of our married life were very different from what I imagined or desired.

One thing was I was not sure if we have had sex or not, because I barely felt him. His disinterest in me was very obvious; I was convinced he didn't like me. I was too shy to talk to him about our sex life, and he was still like a stranger to me. But I strongly felt something was very wrong, which I hoped would get better as we would get to know each other in the days to come. I was mistaken. That familiarity never came in the 34 years that we remained married.

The fleeting intimacy that lasted for barely five minutes on our wedding night didn't happen again till the next month and then once a month if things were good. It went on this way until I conceived my first daughter, which was 20 months after we got married. I can count the times we were intimate in those 20 months. It didn't happen when he was away for some course for two months, one month of fasting was also used as an excuse. Then he got me vaccinated for rubella and said that it was unsafe for six months to get pregnant after the vaccine, so he chose to stay away instead of using some prevention. If I take away these 9 months, at the rate of once a month, the number of times we were intimate in the first 20 months was 11! Every time it was a quick mechanical movement with no hints whatsoever of any tenderness or consideration to me. I didn't experience any pleasure which I could associate with sexual intimacy; he would disengage before that point. After that we had sex for two more times when my daughter was 18 months old. This time I conceived my second daughter. After that he never touched me in the 29 more years we remained married.

Little things like holding hands, doing things together just for the sake of spending time with each other, or saying little meaningless endearments to each other never, ever happened. Whenever I tried, he would never reciprocate which left me feeling unwanted and insulted, I felt my heart breaking every time, and at last I stopped making any effort. This made me very unhappy. As time passed, I learned to make peace with the nature of this relationship, and I stopped thinking about my likes, dislikes, or my feelings. My marriage became my responsibility and duty, so I had to do the best I could because I felt I had no other option. So I, alone, (I say alone because I never felt he ever tried to make me feel happy) assumed the duty of working for the survival of this marriage by trying to make him happy. Little did I know at that time that I would be left exhausted in this task because I was not a man!

As I am writing this, I am wondering why I didn't do anything about this horrible situation! Why didn't I seek help or share my problems with anyone? To be honest I did spend countless nights crying and worrying about the heartbreak and pain I experienced, but in my mind, there didn't seem to be a way out. My mother had been operated on for breast cancer on the third day after my wedding. After that, she was in very poor health physically and very fragile emotionally. I couldn't bear to burden her with my baggage. Given the sexual nature of the problem, I thought it was inappropriate to discuss with the male members of my family, my father and brother. So I kept quiet.

This happened for so long that a point came when I began to see everything as the result of what I was worth. I felt I should try to prove myself worthy of his love if I wanted the marriage to continue... and I wanted this marriage to work at all costs. I should be more understanding towards his weakness (at one point he told me he was abused as a child and as result he was asexual). At that time I worked as hard as I could to please him, but as they say I was walking on eggshells all of the time, never knowing what would upset him.

The decision to carry on and not seek help is probably the biggest mistake I have ever made. It was hard work, but I have forgiven myself now. I had to forgive myself because that was the best I could think of at that time. I was a naïve young inexperienced girl with dreams of raising a loving family with no idea that monsters were real! Though I will continue to pay the price for as long as I live, I have forgiven my innocent naïve self.

Fast forward to our 28th wedding anniversary. At this time, life appeared settled in our relationship and otherwise too. I had made peace with my almost sisterly relationship with him. Both of us were working; I worked a half day, he worked a full day, and as he is a very ambitious writer, he would spend remaining time writing or meeting writer friends. We would frequently go out for book launches and literary gatherings. His work-related responsibilities took him away on frequent travels for days at a time. As he was fond of travelling, so many times he would add weekends to extend his travel plans. I have never accompanied him on these travels; he always chose to travel alone.

Money was not a problem; we were quite comfortable. He became mild in his temper, though I must say as long as he was well attended, and I made sure he was at all times. I tried to take care of his clothes, food, all the chores relating to children and the house--in short all the uninteresting and mundane chores to ensure that nothing disturbed him in his work.

I began to believe my compliance, my hard work with children, the house, and him paid off, meaning, I was able to salvage my marital life by sacrificing my personal fulfillment and happiness. I was the good woman in my story who was selflessly working to help her writer/doctor husband achieve greatness, being happy in his happiness, experiencing success in his success. I thought that by not being demanding, with a lot of patience and sacrifice on my part, I was able to keep my family intact, my children secure and respected in society. I used to think it was not a bad bargain!

So back to our 28th anniversary. He didn't show up in time for the anniversary dinner and called in to say that something very urgent came up. Though I did feel hurt, I was my usual understanding self, so this was soon forgotten. On the fourth day after the missed anniversary dinner, I woke up in the middle of the night and realized he was not on his bed or in the washroom. I went out and heard him talking on phone; the tone was very soft and endearing. When he saw me he ended the conversation and came with me to the bedroom. He seemed too happy and excited to sleep, so he watched TV for some time and talked all the time. It was around 4:00 in the morning that he was able to sleep.

Something in the phone conversation had made me extremely uncomfortable, and I couldn't sleep at all. He told me it was a work related emergency which couldn't have waited till the next day. I was not convinced--I heard him describing the color of his eyes and that was not a work related emergency! For the first time in my life I checked his phone. The last conversation was 90 minutes long, and the caller's name and picture was saved in the address book.

The picture was of a man who looked different... in makeup and with ear studs and a strange pout. I remember my heart missing a beat. I also found the messages that were exchanged before the conversation. They were definitely romantic, praising each other's appearance and planning a "meet up." Next morning I told him what I saw in his phone and questioned about the man and his strange look. He told me that man worked in his office, was in some trouble, and needed help. Noting he said could convince me, and from that moment on, my life changed forever!

Over the next few months I went crazy. I can divide my life into before and after this phone incident. Somehow my eyes and ears, which had been accepting of all the lies up until that point, learned to see and hear better, I began to question his lies (in my mind only, I was not brave enough to confront him till then). I turned into a full time spy, not eating, not sleeping, and only focusing on collecting information. And how successful I was!

What I learned from his old diaries, emails, phone messages, and eavesdropping was unbelievable and more and more mind boggling. The man who claimed to asexual was actually a gay sex addict! When I compiled the list of men with whom he was sexually involved, it reached more than 50! Given that this was happening since he was 20, I am sure it was just the tip of the iceberg. Everything was so astounding and unbelievable, but there was no denying it was all about him, the man I had been living with for 28 years!

One day I gathered all my courage and tried to talk, but he exploded in anger. In the coming days my misery was compounded by his threats to divorce, ridiculing, belittling, and gas lighting me. At this time I found Bonnie Kaye. I learned that I was not a crazy woman; he was the one trying to make me turn into one. After a struggle of around eight months, he at last admitted he was gay. He confessed that one of his friends from his college days was his first lover. He admitted to be in love with a married subordinate soon after we got married. He also confessed to having lovers in different cities where he travelled for work frequently. He accepted all that I discovered or found out, but nothing more. He promised to end everything as we, his family, were the most important people in his life. That day I was able to sleep after a very long time. Bonnie warned me that this wouldn't last, and she was right! It was all a false promise. He never had the intention of keeping his promise; his only purpose was to keep me calm by lying to me in order to continue the facade.

By this time I was in therapy. With help from Bonnie and my therapist, I was beginning to see that ending the marriage was the only possible way out of this situation. My daughters were also a part of this by now. They were going through their own trauma of watching their fathers fall from the high pedestal to unimaginable depths.

I belong to a community where marriage happens only once in a lifetime, and divorce is frowned upon and almost unheard of after such a long married life. My daughters and my brother became my pillars; they were the ones who convinced me that I should leave this relationship. After five years I filed for divorce and became a free woman in March 2019. He had to move out of the house. He went on to character assassination and a maligning campaign against me. Today I am strong enough to let him live in the hell he is trying to create for me, ignore his accusations and along with it people who believe him. I hold my head high today; my truth has made me stronger and his lies are making him weaker with every passing moment.

My therapist tells me that she has seen me transform-- that I have changed myself inside and out. I agree with her. The walk I have walked was through a river of fire, but the silver lining is that I made it to the other side--deeply traumatized, scarred, and wounded--but alive and much stronger.

I will spend the rest of my life tending and caring for the wounds of a lifetime. It is not easy to begin life anew as a divorced woman when you are 57 years old while living in a country with very traditional set of values for women. I now realize the price I paid for keeping that marriage intact was never worth it. Actually it was not a marriage at all--it was never more than a servile bond at any stage. But as they say hindsight is 20/20. I did what I thought was best at that time. I can never turn back the clock to the time and life that could have been. This sense of loss is now a part of me for as long as I live. But coming out alive after swimming through a river of fire is not a mean feat. I believe I have emerged a winner!

I am thankful for the strengths of mind and heart which God has granted me, my family including my daughters and my brother who believed in me and my integrity; these were the strengths which kept me going and were the reason I survived the horror of the so called marriage. I am thankful that I will die as a woman who wanted to live with honesty grace and dignity for whom integrity was more valuable than the glittering sham of married life, who fought with all her might to reclaim her dignity. This is what I wish to leave as legacy in form of memories and lessons for my daughters.

Fiona's Story

My husband and I have been married 24 years. What a journey! I knew him for a year before we married. We met at a big Christian evangelical event in a city in Britain where I lived. I noticed him because he was a Canadian and he carried an air of quiet authority and spiritual devotion. But he also had, what I saw as, a stinking attitude towards women, and I openly challenged him on that. That was when he first noticed me. I was hooked and so was he. We were both fundamentalist Christians in our 30s – passionate about the Bible and our beliefs and wanting to lead 'godly', meaningful lives.

On our first date I asked him outright if he was gay, as it had been on my mind. (In his 'testimony' at one of the churches in my city, he had spoken of a 'perverse lifestyle' that God had rescued him from.) In reply he told me he had at one time wondered if he was gay, but God had healed him, and we need never speak of it again. He held my hand as we walked, and my heart melted. Men were rarely interested in me – I was shy and awkward. I felt incredibly lucky when John wanted to date me. From the get-go he made it clear that we were headed for marriage, and I was happy with that. I quickly and whole heartedly fell in love and pictured spending the rest of my life with him.

Our whole courtship was distant. Not only did we live several hours apart and have only short visits together, but he was keen to keep things 'pure'. He told me he didn't want to 'defraud' me, and that once we were married, he'd be able to open his heart and body fully to me but not until then. He wanted our first kiss to be after the wedding! I told him that was ridiculous! So, he agreed and gave me long, passionate, arousing kisses when we were engaged but, strangely, they ended on the day we married.

A week before our wedding day in the hot summer of 1996 he injured his back. I took his emotional withdrawal and solemnness as indicators of the physical pain he was in. But with hindsight, I realize that he 'disappeared' then, and has never returned. He was at the wedding of course, but he was only there in body and that is how it has been ever since. The closeness that he had promised me – of there being "nothing between us now" – never happened. On the second day of our honeymoon, he said he needed a break from sex. He wanted a week off. I wept and wept. I had never slept with a man before and had waited with great anticipation for my honeymoon. It was dismal. We flew to Canada for the remainder of the honeymoon so I could meet his family, and I had a strong knowing deep inside that he didn't want to be with me. He spoke a lot, when he spoke at all, of his dearest friend, Steve, and how much he missed him. I knew he cared more for Steve than for me, his new bride. Years later I read in his journal that Steve had been his first real crush.

John's emotional distance, his refusal to acknowledge, affirm or compliment me, and his reluctance to have sex with me, were agonizing for me as a young wife. But whenever I tried to talk to him about it, he had subtle ways of convincing me that I was unstable, or imagining things, or demanding too much of him. He told me, "If you are unhappy then you are the one with the problem – don't project it onto me." Alternatively, he would cry and guilt me for not believing God had healed him. He had a strong conviction throughout our marriage that he was the victim; the one I should feel sorry for. I fell for it in the early years.

After 10 months he persuaded me it was time to have a baby. I had always wanted to be a mother, but I also carried a fear that I would be an abuser, just like my own mother had been. However, I eventually agreed. Secretly I hoped that he would finally love me if I bore a child for him, but to my dismay, although he utterly loved 'his' son, it changed nothing in his attitude toward me. (It turned out I was a good mother and I had another child 4 years later. I love my children with every fiber of my being, and I was not an abuser after all. Not that John has ever affirmed my mothering. Once, asked by a friend of mine what he'd be doing for me on Mother's Day, he replied indignantly, 'she's not my mother!' and that was that.)

For 11 years I remained the dutiful wife, desperately trying to make or help this silent, distant man love me. I prayed ardently for him and devoted myself to being the best and most loving I knew how. I was convinced by him that I was the one at fault. He said my 'needs' were like a bottomless pit, and that only God could meet them, and that it was unhealthy that I was looking to him to fulfil them. I spent years in counselling and worked relentlessly at my faults and failings and my mental health. My goal was to be a better wife to him and a better mother to my two sons.

Then, on our 11th wedding anniversary, I planned a mini weekend away for just the two of us. It was only the second time in our marriage that we had been away together as he was never keen on the idea. He was aloof, emotionally distant, disinterested, and made it obvious that he didn't want to be there with me. It was utterly humiliating. Something finally died in me, and I began the process of really grieving the loss of all I'd hoped for in my marriage. I had married John in the belief that God had told me to because he was the perfect choice for me, and I was God's gift to him. I truly thought that any lingering trace of homosexuality in him would grow into heterosexuality because God would cause him to fall in love with me. I had committed myself to a journey of transformation which could only get brighter and more wonderful with time. We were going to prove that God does work miracles! I was convinced that homosexuality was wrong, and that it was the result of psychological and emotional traumas in early childhood. Coming to a crisis on our 11th anniversary was the start of opening my mind to the possibility that what I had believed was flawed, and slowly and very painfully, I began to reevaluate my whole belief system.

I had believed that although we were equal, my husband was the 'head' of our household and I was his helpmate and support. I saw this as God's divine order. I laid my life down hour by hour, 'dying to self' to honour and commend John, to believe in him and see the best in him. I took the blame for my desperate unhappiness and loneliness, for his emotional neglect and distancing. I accepted that he wasn't gay (as he insisted), but rather that I was unhealthily needy. I submitted myself to giving lavishly and forgiving bravely without receiving more than the occasional crumb of affection or acknowledgement. When I eventually came to the end of myself on our 11th anniversary, the agonizing death that happened in me marked the end of that way of living. I just couldn't do it anymore. In fact, I had started to sense that I SHOULDN'T do it anymore, and I intuited that this was the Holy Spirit speaking to me.

John didn't believe I could hear God speak to me because (according to him) God would always speak to the husband first. My role was simply to confirm what he was hearing from God. He also said that God 'hated' divorce, and so he had sworn to me that we would NEVER speak of it, just as we would never speak of his homosexual feelings of the past. For me to vocalize anything to do with us separating or John's failure as a husband meant that I was listening to Satan, and that the spirit of Jezebel was speaking through me. In his journal he described me as having 'given herself over to the demons', and he wrote that I was almost beyond saving! I wish I could say that this enraged me or made me laugh, but the reality was that I cared very much what he thought of me and feared that there might be some truth in it.

My new season, that started back in 2007 on our anniversary weekend, was a season of massive change for me. I clung to my faith like a limpet and cried out to God for help and guidance through my many days and nights of tears. Truly, I grieved the loss of all my hopes and dreams for this marriage. But also, I opened myself to 'hear' God for myself and in new ways. Some very clear guidelines emerged for me which helped me start to dismantle my unhealthy codependency with John. First, my inner voice told me to withdraw emotionally from him, and to set healthy boundaries around my precious heart. This involved me learning to change how I spoke to him – no longer was I to share my thoughts and feelings with him (which he never did with me), no longer was I to call him by names of endearment (which he also never did with me), nor was I to spend time trying to understand him (which had taken up far too much of my brain space) and I was only to answer him simply without elaborating on what I thought (as he dismissed and ignored my attempts at conversation anyway.) Also, I refused all affections from him – his creepy hugs and his grandma pecks on my cheek. If I'd allowed him to continue with those, he'd have justified himself that we had a perfectly healthy marriage! Not on your life Mister! As for sex, he did suggest it just once more – a monthly initiative that had to be entirely his idea – but when I refused, he never repeated the invitation... to this very day! (No doubt it was a huge relief to him not to have to perform his duty in that department ever again.) You know, part of me still clung to the hope that he would notice how distant I'd become, that he'd miss me and that he'd reach out for me ... I still secretly hoped that there might be some kind of healing in our relationship. I was just not ready yet to give up on us.

By 2012, I realized that not only was there still no change in him, but that he was <u>never going to change</u>; he was never going to love me, and he was never going to be attracted to me. What I still couldn't understand was why. I decided to seek some counselling to help me determine what I needed to do next. I could see that I had become way more independent and 'strong'. I'd even gone back to college, got training and started a job. Having been a stay-at-home Mum for 13 years I finally had my own means of support. I had regained some of my self-respect, and I had begun a journey of reconsidering my understanding of homosexuality. I no longer believed in 'love the sinner, hate the sin', because I no longer saw sexual orientation as sin. I recognized that being gay was not a person's choice; it was usually in them from before they were born and was as natural to them as being attracted to men was to me. Yet, it may sound strange to you, but it still came as a shock to me when my counsellor told me that I needed to consider that John was well and truly gay – she said it was abnormal for any heterosexual man not to ask for sex for 5 years! Somehow John seemed asexual more than anything else, and he was also so opposed to homosexuality, so I was confused. There was no indication of him being in relationship with anyone else, or even fancying anyone else... he seemed to be without attraction, in fact he seemed like a dead man walking – not really alive inside at all. I actually kind of wished he'd fall in love with a guy, so I'd have some evidence of who he really was.

It was at that time, by some extraordinary 'coincidence' that a dear Mennonite woman put a book in my hands called 'The Gay Husband Checklist,' written by Bonnie Kaye. Oh my! The light suddenly went on, and despite John being so firmly closeted in his denials, it dawned on me like a ton of bricks that he had never stopped being gay! This was why the marriage had failed! I was right, he was never going to change. Eureka!

My counsellor pressed me to consider divorcing him. However, I could not find my peace to do this – namely because of my two sons who, I believed, needed a stable home and adequate financial security. I have wrestled over this so many times, and struggled with other peoples' points of view on the subject, but at the end of the day I could only find inner peace (which indicated to me that I was hearing God for my situation) in a decision to stay; just until both my boys had graduated high school... with the caveat that if it became unbearable for me or my children in the home (or I met someone else), I would of course pursue divorce. And so, I stayed. I had him move (very angrily) to another bedroom and began to explain to my boys what was happening and what the future would look like. When they were young, I told them that grown up brothers and sisters don't share a bedroom, and because Mum and Dad were not like a married couple, but like siblings, we needed to have separate bedrooms. As they got older, I told them more, bit by bit. When my eldest was 18 I told him, his Dad was gay.

He wasn't at all surprised, but equally he didn't really care. Young people are so much more broad-minded than I was at that age. A year later he told his younger brother. Neither of my sons holds it against their Dad; he has always been a pretty good and loving father. However, there is no doubt he would have been a much better father had he loved and respected their mother. Loathing his wife and withholding from her affected his parenting. Perhaps they may never understand what the price has been for their Mum, but I have chosen to let that go. I have my own journey, my own pain and my own healing. They are not responsible for me, but I know my boys love me dearly. This summer my youngest son graduated. Three days later, after the celebrations were done, I told his father I'd started divorce proceedings. To my astonishment he has received the news with what I can only describe as excitement! I've never known him this happy, or this kind to me in the 24 years we've been married! He makes it very clear to others that the divorce is not his choice, but I've given him a get-out-of-jail-free card, and he can't contain his relief. He has stunned me by not contesting anything but responding to all my lawyer's requests as speedily as his little legs will carry him! Who knew!

Christians often have very strong opinions about homosexuality. Such a 'hot potato' topic only adds to the agony of the unfortunate straight Christian woman married to a gay Christian man. I have avoided telling many people who I might have confided in for this very reason. Why, O why, do they feel the need to give me a sermon on the subject? I was hurting enough without that being added. Lots of people, Christian or otherwise, feel sorry for John and tell me so. It used to depress me, now it just makes me angry. He's a grown man living in an embracing western culture in the 21ˢᵗ century – he has no excuses anymore. "Ah", but they say, "He's trapped in the expectations of the church." The church has a lot to answer for and has treated gays appallingly, it is true. Thankfully, in this part of the world, things are starting to change, and men and women can live more openly and honestly as homosexuals. Sadly huge portions of Christian culture still promote patriarchy, giving the husband rights over his wife (however subtly it is expressed) and allowing gay men to 'hide' in gay-straight marriages; actually advocating that such a man is doing the brave and right thing by denouncing his 'natural' yearnings and doing his duty as a husband and a father. This allowed John to use me as his 'beard' for 24 years and made me into the Jezebel; the evil, un-submissive, demanding woman. The truth of the reality of our marriage was to be forfeited for the bigger so-called Truth of 'God's holy way' which could not include any suggestion of homosexuality or divorce. John's denial and abhorrence of his true feelings was commended and was ministered to behind closed doors that I was never allowed to see or know about. I hope that you understand now that I do not blame John for being gay. But I do blame him for denying it, for refusing to be honest with me and for scapegoating me with the blame for the failure of the marriage. And I blame his church culture for promoting that kind of dishonesty.

I would hate to leave you with the impression that I had no support from other Christians. Although none may have understood what I was going through, some carefully chosen friends provided a non-judgmental, listening ear and affirmed me, my processing and my ultimate decisions, without questioning. Some even read Bonnie's monthly newsletters just so they could understand my troubles better. They backed me wholeheartedly. They allowed me to weep and wail, to express my rage and my despair, and they said, "We believe in you" and "You are a good Mum"; things that I really needed to hear. They prayed for me and with me when I wanted it. It is a journey we walk alone, in so many ways, but I'll be forever grateful for the few who have stood by my side through thick and thin, even though they couldn't really understand what I was facing.

Do I wish I'd never married him? I don't see any point in thinking about it; all the difficulties and traumas of the marriage have been the ground for tremendous spiritual, emotional and personal growth for me. Plus, I gained a whole new life in Canada, and my 2 wonderful sons. Do I wish he'd been honest with me when he'd started to realize that he still wasn't attracted to women, and that my physical body grossed him out? Absolutely, yes! That would have been the manly thing to do, and it would have been the kindest to me, who had never been at fault in this whole mess. Am I angry that he scapegoated and blamed me for the failure in the marriage? Yes, I'm furious! He has been an immature, selfish asshole, and he needs to grow up and take responsibility for his own stuff. Am I going to be ok? I believe I am. The struggles of the last 24 years have helped me mature, helped me learn to love and care for myself, helped me come to value who and what I am, and have relieved me of all my dependency on him. Will my kids be ok? I truly hope so. They have been my foremost concern since their dear little bodies were placed in my arms all those years ago in the delivery room. I have sought to be honest (yet impartial) when explaining the marriage to them, and I have tried to keep a stable environment for them to grow up in and to prepare them for the future.

I have not lost my faith, through all this, but it has changed almost beyond recognition. I have come to a place where I believe God loves all people; race, gender, age, and sexual orientation really don't matter, but truth-telling does. I am invited to a partnership with the Divine, and my thoughts and needs really matter – decision making is a thing we do together now; gone are the patriarchal days when I would wait on Him to know what I should do, just like I did with my husband. And yes, I believe Creator is as much female as male; in fact, I am made in Her image, and I am good... body and soul! A middle finger up to patriarchy and to Christian men and gays who think they are entitled to treat women as 'less' than themselves.

In the next few weeks, our house will be sold, John will go his way and I will go mine. My sons will choose who they want to live with. A whole new life awaits me, a life I've dreamed of for years and years! Gosh, I'm nervous about starting afresh as a single woman again after so long! But it's the next step and it's necessary and I have a whole network of good women who are cheering me on.

Catherine's Story

Things people do not want to talk about: Gay men marrying straight wives; living the greatest Lie unknowingly…

I live in The Netherlands, a country that is known for ages for its 'tolerance,' but how much tolerance does it take to install a lockdown on truth being told? I am 65 years now and 3.5 years out. My life story is nowhere welcome in these days of glorifying homosexuality as them being almost the new Jesus. I, as a straight wife, am not heard in this 'tolerant' society. See no evil, hear no evil; is that the equivalent of being tolerant?

On August 11, 2016, just after we celebrated our 36th wedding anniversary together with our three children, I received a notification on Facebook that my husband liked a certain site. I was curious what he had liked and was baffled when it turned out to be a site where men in scarce underwear were displaying themselves. Something very dark stared me in the face and enveloped my being. I showed it to him and asked what that was all about and he answered with a faint smile, "That was a mistake; the guy has the same name as someone I search for to be my guide for my travel to Asia." I answered, "No Eric, you liked that site, apparently you still need to lie. When you are ready to tell me that truth about yourself I will see you in my study. He did not sleep in the marital bed that night. The next morning he confessed to being gay, accompanied by another lie that 'he did not know he was gay'…

You see, I asked several times during my marriage, whether he was gay. The reason for that question being that he left me in my bed after the three children were born (he had wanted 6 children but I refused). He always vehemently denied being gay, got angry and/or did not speak to me anymore that day. The shroud of gaslighting was installed from the beginning. He had a younger gay brother that always openly lived his life. He was always negative about him, giving him nicknames and mimicking him as he was quite effeminate. He himself appeared to be the opposite and very 'straight,' so every time the question appeared inside my head I compared him to his brother and dismissed the possibility of him being gay. I could not come up with a reason as to why a gay man would want to marry a straight woman…so I believed him when he denied being gay.

Until 2008, we were materially blessed having started our own company and working diligently together. Looking back I know what characterized him always; it was never enough. After 2008 we nearly lost it all due to him turning down a good offer to sell off the company, bad investments, bad decisions, and he would never take my advice. I always felt there was a nasty little kid living inside of him.

In 2005 he organized a second vow ceremony in Croatia as we were married 25 years that year. We took 30 guests on a cruise. When it was over, I told him I'd never felt as alone as during that cruise. He was constantly elsewhere and busy to film for the cruise reunion party that he already had in mind. I was left by myself and everybody else had their partner. After I pulled him from his closet and the veil of dissociation was slowly lifted from my consciousness, while looking back realized that already then he must have been engaged in meetups with very young men. The 2nd vow ceremony was a smoke and mirror action and I indeed believed myself to be so lucky I had a very good husband. The sex....well that was non-existent, but I loved him. Even after our kids left the house and I asked for physicality again, he said he would call me a gigolo. I was dumbstruck but the mind hack he had been doing for then over 25 years was so ingrained that I could find fault with myself only for him not wanting me.

He always was projecting outward into the future and always focused on getting attention to the max. I remember him putting on a speech that never stopped at a dinner party. Guests were starting to be embarrassed and I knocked him against the ankles, but he did not take it; he was glorified by himself in the moment until he was finally interrupted by the host. I knew then I would remember this moment later because it really characterizes his personality.

Looking back I went in shock when I realized that my reality for 37 years had been an Illusion and was therefore ready to be even more manipulated by him. Five weeks after I pulled him from his closet, an apartment was bought where I was to live. It was much too expensive as it turned out later and after three years. I had to leave it again and find a rental place. He still lived in the house where we raised our children and a young Chinese refugee (then 31 years, he was then 69 years) who took my space in the bed one week after I had moved out. The friends stayed quiet. He went on a charming offensive right away--and he succeeded.

I also accepted that he stayed in the house where I had lived for 30 years for the last Christmas and that I was to go to our little homestead on a Greek isle that had no heating all by myself! But I was sure I did not want to pretend with this last 'married' Christmas that we were a happy family any longer. He let me sign a document to settle financial matters (I had little money of my own) in which he arranged that I would be permanently financially dependent on him in spite of the fact that the house was in my name. I was manipulated again, only now financially.

Two years after I left the house I had gathered my own mind back together and went to see a lawyer. Now, 3.5 years out of a marriage to a gay man and 70.000 euro's later, I am finally divorced from a gay man that intentionally went into a marriage with a straight woman. He admitted that he had had gay encounters before we were married. Today he tells people 'he did not know' to play upon the emotions of compassion of people he "confides in." Those people sent me cards saying they found him very courageous to be so open, but he still plays with people. They were their last cards for me. They all cheer this coward of a man for his guts of coming out but I gave him that gift because I pulled him out. That at last he can be himself is my last gift to him whereas I have been abused on all levels of humanity by this exploitative man that destroyed all I ever cared for—namely, my family.

My first granddaughter is on her way to this world but she will know that granny chose to not set eyes on grandfather ever again.

The experience of straight wives is severely overlooked in today's societies by the aggressive activist attitude of the LHBTIQ community. Whereas the coming out is celebrated the experience of the straight wife is overlooked and passed by. She is showered with all the questions and judgments that they should have asked the gay husband because she did not know! She was always just a chess piece on his chessboard and she did not know she was being played. How cruel is his intention to hold for another living being and what a foundation to spawn new life on into this world.

Straight wives are abused on all human levels: physical, emotional, mental and spiritual. The burden is almost unbearable, and yet straight wives are surrounded by a deafening silence whereas their former husbands embark all too readily on their gay life style and move on supported by all kinds of gay institutions and social help with the help of the media. None of it exists for the abused straight spouses; they belong to the last ignored consequences of a patriarch society where anything female is diminished and of less value than the (gay) male experience.

With all the propagated new lifestyle of "we are all fluid," a new generation of abused straight women is on the way. This will make it easier for gay men to hide behind a mask. I would never have chosen to raise a family with a gay man of my own free will, but I was never given a choice by him. Is this Freedom of Will not in our constitutions? So why is it overlooked so easily in divorce when a person has been intentionally deeply abused and misled by another for his own selfish reasons? Do you really believe we live in a so much propagated new 'inclusive' society?

Bianca's Story

A married person coming out as homosexual is not an individual matter, but a family matter. When deception is discovered, the wife, husband, and children are hurt.

When I met Steve in college, I was very much in love. During the first years of marriage, we were poor but mostly happy. After trying so hard to have babies, we had our daughter, Kristy, and eighteen months after that our son Steven. During this time, we were in Merritt Island pursuing professional jobs and working both to support our family. I quit working to fully enjoy and care for both kids while Steve studied for his master's degree.

From the beginning, I sacrificed my profession for him so he could grow in his career while I would be a good mother to the kids. Money was tight, but my father always helped me. As all young families were busy all those years, and my husband was absent most of the time. When he started to work for UPS, I was alone all of the time with two babies. I knew something was missing, and feeling so depressed, I decided to move to Miami.

By surprise, Michael came into our lives after seven months of pregnancy. Again, my father gave us the apartment to live in. Money was always a problem to us then.

With three babies, I knew we had to do whatever we could to keep our marriage together. One night there was a phone call from a crying woman that made me realize something was wrong in our marriage. I ignored this call for the sake of our children.

Steve was an expert of living two separate lives—one as a husband, father, and church professional, and the other as an anonymous gay man. He learned how to compartmentalize these feelings and actions. I am convinced he had the ability to use these two personalities in order to survive.

Those years were busy with sports practices, games, retreats, and religious socialization. We lived in the same house, but we were definitely drifting apart. I felt increasingly unsupported and frustrated by our lack of communication and closeness.

We moved to Miller Drive, and I was so busy raising three children and assisting them in sports while Steve was flying long runs and going for his PH.D (doctorate) degree. I was always alone and sacrificing myself to be a better mother and homemaker. Saturdays and Sundays we were introduced to UPS flight schedules. I knew something was wrong because my husband was flying more often away from home. However, to others we appeared as the "perfect couple." Everyone thought we had it all: business, success, church roles, wealth, community recognition, expensive cars, and world travel. However, there was something wrong with each of us because we felt alone in our house, even when we were together.

When my father became sick, there was tension all of the time between us. I went to visit my father alone daily to watch him deteriorate each day. Our isolation was growing more and more. When my father died, my grief was unbearable, but I didn't have support from my husband. I felt abandoned for the first time.

Within a few weeks, Steve became another person. I missed my father so much. He was the one who held the family together. This is when I felt more isolated and alone than ever. I tried to compensate by working harder and taking trips to my home in Lima to be with relatives and friends.

I felt so isolated and struggling in our efforts to stay together. As months passed, I became resentful that my husband would not care for the house or the repairs of the house while he was already living his secret life. I had to create a new life for myself working in the business only to come home and endure the feeling of loneliness and isolation that was present at all times. I never thought that he had secrets, much less that he was living a lie each day. How did I miss the loss of weight, the change to younger clothing, the pills for low male hormones, testosterone, the facial creams, the new food habits, the new single male friends, the out at midnights, bisexual group encounter videos, the lies, the excuse that our children were lazy and with no responsibilities, the inexplicable stress he was always feeling in his mind.

Finally, the moving out for a while because he felt disappointment from our children. He said he needed the distance in order to sort his feelings out. I knew something was wrong, but I was afraid to know the truth.

I finally came to the conclusion that I was used not only as a care giver bearing his children, but also as his companion and social partner. Being a traditional wife, I provided him with a safe environment and image to his career, good money saving household, protection of his sexual orientation with a family, avoidance of fear of losing touch with the children, not to mention protection of his fundamental religious convictions.

Then Steve said he did not love me anymore when he had deceived me for 31 years. How many of those years did he have homosexual tendencies? I see clearly how I was. I was torn apart totally with the invasion of his boyfriend into the household; if I knew this before I could have been suspicious of his other "strange' relationships. The way he disclosed his homosexuality to the kids and me was very abrupt and negative with a deliberate deceit. He hid it for years, with no fidelity or honesty, followed by an explosion of his truth. How brutal it was.

Suddenly his wife and children are in the closet too. It seems like I was watching a horror movie only that this is real. This cannot be happening to us. I went into shock, denial was my first reaction. I lost 20 pounds. I had been unable to eat and sleep properly. I went to the Emergency Room for immense anxiety. My health is currently fragile. Meanwhile after his disclosure, my life must go on as before on the surface. I keep struggling to make some resemblance to a normal routine. I was disoriented in carrying this big trauma. While he says now to the kids that he was struggling with me, what he should have said was that he was struggling with his homosexual feelings, his low self-esteem, loss of trust, love, and respect for his wife and kids.

After a year and a half of disclosure, he decided to seek counseling because he wanted to heal "relationships." WHY? Isn't he happy with his gay life or is his uncertain future making him buy land and farms? This is a common fear. He just ended a life we built together.

I still treasure the memories of our family. They are not struggles to me—but rather the struggle of him not being honest with himself. He put words of excuse to his gay activities by saying he did not love me anymore. HOW HUMILIATING THIS IS TO ME, AFTER GIVING HIM THREE LOVELY KIDS AND SACRIFICING MY LIFE TO OUR MARRIAGE that he used as a cover for his homosexual activities. I feel betrayed—it is very unfair, and he said the judge will make it all fair. How could this be when he started being so unfair since he betrayed and deceived us?

Steve's shame and guilt made him humiliate me. We are all angry with him; the whole family suffered the effects of his secrecy. We have lived tormented over the basic questions of ethics, values, and beliefs.

We feel repression and frustration with each other. I am married to a gay man...we feel a stigma; we carry his stigma too. This is probably why I tried to remain married for a while. I believe the marriage is over. There is so much psychological damage that we all have and the unhappiness that we feel for him.

Facing all of these realities is hard for the entire family. We have sadness and a sense of monumental loss. All of my life plans have changed. All my dreams, future plans, retirement together, travel together, mutual love and support, growing old together, hopes and expectations are dashed. An immense disappointment I bear because Steve did not hold onto the marriage.

I feel that the loneliness of my situation is grossly unfair. Why me? What did I do to deserve this? I feel angry because Steve used me to hide his life without my permission. We were the normal happy couple while he went out with his secret. I just have to take one day at a time, my home life has been disrupted, health concerns left me emotional scars, and trust and security are gone. I am a giant black hole.

The kids and I need years of transition to recover the crisis of trauma, abandonment, insecurity, and conflicts of loyalty. We hope to find peace of mind and find wholeness again. Finally I am going to end my story with my prayer of every night: God grant me the serenity to accept things that I cannot change, courage to change things I can, and wisdom to know the difference.

Paula's Story

If I am honest with myself, the signs were all there. In the clear 20/20 vision of hindsight, the gay cards were on the table early in our relationship. This is that bombshell in a nutshell. I now know that the first time he lied to me was during our first conversation, at the Teachers' Institute Day to kick off the 1989-1990 school year. No, he did not tell his last principal to forget extending his contract. No sane person does that. She chose not to extend his contract, just like many other supervisors to follow.

I had just returned from yet another summer in Germany. West Germany was flush with money in 1989, and the country was happily spending cash to train teachers from other countries to spread the gospel of Goethe, Schiller, and Beethoven. I converted in high school, got my BA in German, and managed to land a job teaching my favorite language in a suburban Chicago high school. Life was good. At 34, I owned a townhouse, a snappy European car, plenty of nice clothes, and managed to get to Europe nearly every summer. Sometimes I travelled for pleasure, sometimes as a tour guide, and other times, as is in the summer of 1989, on scholarship to study. Life was pretty good.

There was, at that time, no one special in my life. I had had one very long-term relationship and many shorter ones, but no one had decided to choose me as a life partner, nor I them. At times, it had bothered me, but by the time I met him, I really did not care. I had come to terms with life as a single woman, and I was just fine with that. It would be my cat, Winston, and I against the world.

He walked into my classroom, looking for a Spanish teacher. My first words to him were, "She's down the hall." When he turned to leave, I noticed that cute, little butt. Perfect. He was easy on the eyes, and I remember saying to myself to calm down. He is probably taken. At our first department meeting, I noticed that his last name was an ethnic match to mine. We both had, or at least appeared to have, the same heritage. An interest in language, same background, this could be an interesting year.

As it turned out, he and I were scheduled for the same lunch. Teachers select tables in the lunchroom like congregants select pews in church. Once you choose one, it becomes your permanent seat. Woe unto an interloper, you shall endure the "teacher look" for that period. We chose a spot in the center of the room. This was where I was fed the first lies, though at the time, I was so smitten, I did not see the forest for the trees. All I knew was that there was this guy…

We sat together for weeks. We seemed to connect on every level. Were he a regular guy, the date would have happened within the first month of the school year. Nothing. Not even a slight suggestion. He talked about going to his brother's wedding, the shoes he bought for the event (red flag), how he disliked his future sister-in-law. Nothing. His class reunion came and went. Nothing. But I am a very patient person. It would happen.

Finally, as Christmas approached, he asked if I had ever dined in a particular Mexican restaurant. No, I had not. It was not in my neck of the suburbs. I had never heard of it. So… it was set. A date! A real live date! It was set for the evening of the day we began our Christmas break. This is when I began to learn that "punctual" is not in his vocabulary. He is not even fashionably late. He is just late. I taught German. My trains run on time. He was a Spanish teacher. Mañana was his word. The day ended at 3:00. I waited in my dark, empty classroom until well after 4:00 for him to finally walk upstairs to start our date. Why? He was involved in his evaluation conference. He was tangling with our department chair, Dr. Bob, a crazy, vindictive, little Napoleon. They were two peas from the same pod. It did not go well. I knew it would not go well. Rumors were swirling around the department that he and Dr. Bob were at each other's throats. Of course, in his mind, or at least, out of his mouth, all was well.

We stopped at his condo before I, yes, I, drove to the restaurant, an hour away. It was snowing, and I did drive a car designed to be operated at the Arctic Circle, so that is how I justified the fact that I was the chauffeur for the evening. I recall little of the date. I think the food was good. I know we talked and talked. I dropped him in his parking lot at the end of the evening. There was no kiss goodnight, no invitation to come inside; I just drove home. The weather was not good, so I simply assumed that he thought it best for me to get on the road. I had another 40 minutes of travel ahead of me.

Somewhere during that evening, we decided to spend New Year's Eve together at my place. I asked my father for advice concerning the dinner. He suggested an Italian dish that I had mastered. All men like pasta, right? I later learned that he loathes pasta. He is not like other men. He was supposed to arrive at 6:00. Dinner was in the oven and set to be served by 6:45. At 6:10, my phone rang. He was running late, like well over an hour late. Are you kidding me? Normal women would have been angry, but I sucked it up. It was going to be a late night, but it was New Year's

Eve. It is supposed to be late. I know we talked about foreign language textbooks for hours. He claims that there was a passionate kiss at midnight. I remember nothing other than he left in the wee hours of the New Year, and I went to bed, alone, thinking that I might have found the "one." Oh, yes, I was in lust.

The next time we spoke was when school started again. To say that I was disappointed would be an understatement. We still ate lunch together, but that was it. No more talk of getting together again. Of course, he had his own problems. He decided to buy a new condo before he knew his job status for the next year. He had been warned about our DC. He had not only tangled with him, but he had unhappy parents of students, a terrible sign. The handwriting was on the wall. There would be no contract renewal. He was out of a job. I would find out later, that this was a pattern. He could not hold a job because he never played nice in the sandbox. He wanted to be king of the playground and keep all the toys for himself.

Throughout the next several months, I was there, his good friend, supporting him as he went from job interview to job interview, always claiming that he was the "lead" candidate but never landing the position. I dutifully went to his condo daily to talk over his dilemma. I listened as he read whole papers he had written as an undergrad. I was regaled with evidence of deus ex machina in Molière's, *Tartuffe*, TWICE. (Who saves undergrad papers? Who reads them aloud to people? I do not even have my master's thesis anymore.) I filled his fridge with groceries and cooked for him. I cleaned his place while he went to work at a part time gig at a furniture store. I bought his cigarettes. I paid when we went out. I tried.

Then one evening, in September, he announced that he wanted to end our friendship. He thought that I was getting too involved. (I was.) He only wanted me as a friend. I am seven years older than he, and that bothered him. I cleared out my things from his condo, drove home, sobbing, and that was that. Move on...

Which is what I did. I moved on. I don't know what we had during that year. We were certainly never romantically involved. He never touched me. If I even so much as rubbed my hand against him, he recoiled. I kept waiting for the kiss, anything physical, and it never happened. Most other guys would have swooped in, but not this guy. Of course, he had been in the seminary. He had spent years preparing to become a celibate Catholic priest. They must have taught him something. Oh, yes, they taught him.

My gap year from him was busy. I had been selected to spearhead a program integrating education and technology. This was cutting edge stuff in 1990. I received a state-of-the-art computer and all sorts of ancillaries for the program from corporate sponsors. These took up precious space in my townhouse. It was time to move. I needed space and wanted to get closer to the school. I was extremely involved in the music program of a local university. I sang with the chorus, was a member of a grad school ensemble, and was the rehearsal soprano soloist. I was NEVER home on Monday evenings during concert season. I traveled. I had friends. He was in my rear-view mirror.

One Monday evening, very close to the day I was to move, I was home. Don't ask why. Maybe the rehearsal ended early. Maybe it was cancelled. I don't remember, but I was home when the phone rang. This was before caller

ID was ubiquitous. I picked up, and yes, it was his voice. He purposely selected to call on a Monday in the hope of getting my answering machine. That way if I wanted to tell him where to go and how to get there, he would not have to hear it. He was nervous but pleasant, saying that he missed me, and that he would like to try again. Would I be up for another dinner at the restaurant where we had our first "date?" He had a job. He could afford a relationship. I was hesitant but agreed. Why not?

Of course, I had to drive over to his place. I knew the drill. He proudly showed me his clean condo. He had hired a cleaning service to take care of that chore, one that used to be mine, and he had a gift for me – a pink rose. Oh, yes, my little heart melted. Dinner and conversation followed. We went back to his place, talked a bit, and he walked me to his door. There was a single kiss. No, it was a peck. That was it. You would think that there would have been some passion, some I missed you. Nope. A peck.

Over the ensuing weeks, he called nightly. My new townhouse was close to his home, so he came over often. He spent hours on my computer. I sat on the floor and watched. Stupid woman. I often slept while he researched genealogy, something that would later become the bane of my existence. He occasionally kissed me. That was it. I tried. I gave him oral sex. He loved that, but I got nothing in return. When I asked, he said that he was a nice Catholic boy, and he wanted to wait until he married. He was polite and respectful.

We decided to marry after attending a wedding. We were certain that we could pull off a better party than the one his cousins had hosted. They served pizza and hot apple cider. We could definitely top that. There was no getting on one knee, no big ring reveal, just we can throw a better party. This was going to be his show. He loved musicals (HUGE red flag) and directed them as a teacher. Our wedding was a show he wrote, directed, and in which he starred. He did have to try to share the spotlight with my mother. The stage was not big enough for the two of them. There was blood. I was a bit player at my own wedding.

Nothing happened on our wedding night. He was too tired. We had slept together for months. We occupied the same bed. Nothing. I tried. God, how I tried. Nothing. Good Catholic boys wait until the marriage is signed and sealed. That was always his answer to my question. Finally, when we checked into our hotel in Cancun, the relationship was consummated. Let's call it the proverbial, wham, bam, thank you ma'am. He was as awkward as they come (pun intended). How could he be 30 years old and not have a clue?

We settled into married life. I did expect sex. I expected that he would expect it. I was frequently rebuffed. He was too tired, or he had some ache or pain, or there was some other complaint. We wanted a family. I was 37, and he was 30. We had to get busy. Time was a wasting. The only way that the family would happen was... drum roll, please... sex. It turns out that he was a morning kind of guy. All guys wake up ready to go, so this was convenient. He did not have to try. I was pregnant by Christmas.

Within the first three years of our marriage, we were blessed with two beautiful sons. He was a good daddy. He played on the floor with them. He bathed them. He read them stories. We went on family outings. Intimacy was a scheduled thing, but I assumed that most couples with young kids did that. I worked full time, as well as ran the household. I was tired. Everything seemed normal.

He did have gay friends. One was his former boss, and the other was part of a team, to which he belonged, negotiating a new teachers' contract. Friends, colleagues. Nothing more. They appeared at the house periodically. Sometimes, he went out with them. I thought nothing of it. Then, they vanished. His friends always disappeared over time. I brought my friends into our relationship. We socialized with them. We vacationed with them. They are still my friends. He brought no one.

Then there were the cards, or I assume what were cards, from Mick. This was the '90s when people still sent greetings in the mail. I recall the envelope with the return address. Remember, I was a German teacher, so anything German catches my attention. I saw the name, a German name, an interesting name. I mentioned that and then asked about this person. He just said that he was some weird, gay guy from college. There would be other cards and letters. I only saw the envelopes, never the contents. He never displayed these cards with others on the mantel. This guy would haunt me.

The babies grew into boys and wanted to do "boy" things. They wanted to ride their bikes, play ball, go swimming. He was not interested. He began to distance himself from us. I did those boy things with our sons. The family outings were less frequent. He complained about doing anything outdoors. He would sometimes accompany us, but over the years, that stopped. He spent more and more time in the office on the computer, with the door closed. It was either work or another degree he needed to advance his career. By then, he was a principal. It was odd, but I assumed that he was doing this for the family. The better the job, the more financially secure our family would be. Too bad he lost those jobs. Every single one of them. In the end, he had a doctorate and nothing to show for it. By the way...do not forget that doctorate. He is always Dr.-- never Mr. He instructed his mother to address our mail with Dr. and Mrs.

Gay reared its ugly, little head in about 2005. We had just moved into a new house. Since our sons were still in elementary school, we had a family email account, for which I was responsible. He hated mail, any kind of mail. It sat in piles for months on the desk or on the screen for years. I sorted through the daily emails, deleting junk, putting other bits into folders, and telling everyone what was waiting for their attention. I started to notice emails from dating sites, such as Match.com. While that was strange enough, these were messages from the gay side. When I asked about that because I did not think our junior high boys should see those things, he blew it off, saying that we have a new email account, and these companies are simply looking for hits. He assured me they would stop soon, and they did.

We drifted along. I honestly thought that my marriage was solid. I did not really notice anything amiss because we had been drifting for so long. He lived in the office, staring at a computer screen and listening to musicals. Sex was rare. Kisses were pecks. There were no date nights, though I do remember an anniversary when we spent the night at an adult motel, with a pool in our suite. There were rose petals on the bed, and champagne in a bucket. It appeared so romantic. There was a box from Lover's Lane. Was it a sexy, little nightie? Nope. He bought me a pair of silk pajamas – men's purple, silk pajamas because he thought I would be more comfortable in that. Really???

He then began to complain that the abundance of email prevented him from sitting with me and the boys in the evening. He had to cull the herd in the office and had no time to relax. This was about the time that the first iPad appeared. Those little gizmos are small, portable computers. He could check his email on that device and sit with us in the family room. Christmas gift! He loved it. Unfortunately, instead of reading his email, he started looking for old friends on social media. Remember Mick with the interesting German name? He found him. Friends from the seminary appeared. Guys from a group of high school friends discerning Franciscan priesthood showed up. Gay. Almost every single one of them are gay. He was out with these people often. There were dinners, drinks, all sorts of gatherings of his old friends. I was never included. It was always a guys' night. Wives need not apply.

In June of 2009, he announced that he was not going to spend the 4th of July with us. His friend, Mick, was traveling back home from St. Louis to NYC and would have a layover in Chicago. They were going to meet up and have dinner. What restaurant is open on that holiday of backyard BBQs and picnics? I suggested that, if time permitted, why not bring Mick here for dinner. I always grilled steaks on that day. Funny thing. He thought it was a great idea. Can you say awkward? I got the distinct impression that this guy was looking for a date and got a wife and two kids, instead. Even our sons told him not to bring his friends over. They are all too strange.

Then Rick appeared. For the first time in our marriage, I sensed danger, and I could not even tell you why. He was supposed to be an old friend, though I had never, ever heard his name. No one in his family mentioned him. When I met Rick, he seemed nice enough. He is not overtly, limp-wristed gay, but he was one of those gay old friends and supposedly in a committed relationship. I asked how they know each other. The answer made no sense. A little background would be helpful...

When he decided in high school that he had a vocation to the priesthood, he applied to the archdiocesan seminary in Chicago. He was rejected after the psychological evaluation. I have no idea as to the exact reason. He only said that they were concerned about his relationship with his father, which was problematic. He then hooked up with an individuated Franciscan priest, on staff at his high school. This means that the priest lives alone, and not in community, as is customary. This priest was shepherding several guys through the discernment process. They all celebrated church and Franciscan feasts at the home of this priest with dinner and Mass. Frequently, they all stayed overnight. Let your imagination run wild here.

Rick does not seem to be the priest type, but he claimed he knew Rick from this group. Rick did not even attend the same high school. There is nothing remotely religious about him. I could not see the connection. I would find out later.

For the first time in my life, I saw passion. Whenever, he spoke of Rick, his eyes lit up. He reminded me of a freshman girl, who was just noticed by the senior captain of the football team. He was in a swoon and looked for any excuse to be with this guy. He bought him expensive gifts. He bought him souvenirs from our vacations. I had never seen this behavior before.

And then we were empty nesters…our older son was at the United States Naval Academy in Annapolis, and the younger was attending his father's alma mater, which no longer housed the seminary. On our first evening alone, he announced that he would be watching TV in the nude. Okay. It is your house. Whatever floats your boat, as they say. Years ago, he joked about doing this so that we could have sex in every room of our house. He said he would buy sex toys for fun. Yeah, right. By this time, it was 2013, it had been years since we were intimate. He blamed his performance problems on health issues, including low testosterone. He was drinking heavily by this time and was often passed out in his chair when I came to say goodnight. Sometimes he made it to bed in the wee hours; other times he spent the night in his rocking chair, lights and fireplace blazing until I woke him in the morning. His iPad was always in his lap.

One evening, I walked over to him to kiss him goodnight and looked down at his iPad. There was a picture of an erect penis. Stupid me. I assumed that he had inadvertently photographed his genitalia with his iPad. Why else would that pic be on the screen? He was naked and drunk. Taking that sort of photo would probably be easy. I never said a word. Later, I found out that he had been trading dick pics with online friends.

By this time, he was a school superintendent. He was the top dog. This was his dream job. Of course, one of the unsaid requirements of this position is a family. The sup is the face of the school district to the community. He or she must be a normal person, living a normal life, doing normal things. He needed us to maintain his air of normalcy so that he could relate to the community. We were his cover. He had the wife, who was a retired teacher. He had two sons in college, one at a service academy. He was active in the community, active in our parish. He looked good. Except it was all a façade, and some of those board members started to suspect that something was off. He was hired by a female board. Women and gay guys are often best friends. When men were elected, things went south. They wanted to discuss the district and sports, building initiatives and sports, finances and sports. They asked, "Cubs or Sox?" He would haughtily reply that he does not like sports. He likes musicals and genealogy. The men were put off. He was late to work often (I later discovered red light camera tickets from Rick's neighborhood from times when he should have been in the office.) He did not attend district functions, as requested, especially athletic events. He made some bad hires. He, as I said, does not play nice, and he was not playing nice. A sup sending a cease and desist letter to a board member is not playing nice. His contract was not renewed.

I attributed his increasingly strange behavior at home to the job loss. His overly inflated ego took a real hit. In our 26-year marriage, this was job #5 to slip through his fingers. Now, he was having difficulty finding another job. Positions were available, but he was never the right fit. Then there was his age. At 56, I could see the behavior as a male mid-life crisis. Go out and buy a Porsche. Drive fast and get it out of your system. Too bad none of that sort of thing interested him. Other than genealogy and musicals, nothing interested him. Well, he was interested in himself and Rick. I tried to talk about the problems. I had tried for years. Every time I brought up an issue, he either refused to discuss it or twisted everything around so that I felt a noose tightening around my own neck by the end of the conversation. I felt worse after the discussion than when we had begun. Nothing was ever resolved. He said I was throwing a pity party. I just gave up. This was my lot, a celibate marriage to a man who was more interested in himself than in his family, but we were still holding it together.

I look back on those last years and wonder why I put up with it all. I was committed. I made a promise in front of God, and my family and friends. I never break my promise. I would stay, even though I knew that I did not love him anymore. I hated what he had become. I cringed when I noticed that it was time for him to come home from work. He would put his briefcase down, announce that he had to explode (Do not ask. It is too gross.) and spend the next 20 minutes in the bathroom. Then we would eat our dinner listening to him talking about himself or fielding phone calls and texts. He sat in the family room nightly, surrounded by pillows to block the screens of his iPad and phone while he scrolled and texted. Something was wrong, terribly wrong.

One afternoon, I was having difficulty sending a message with an attachment to a friend. When I finally thought that I had managed to forward it, I checked my sent file to make certain. A strange address caught my eye. It started with M2M4fun, which I later deciphered as, "Man to man for fun." His name with a receipt for a purchase was there. I knew that he had multiple addresses. That had started several years ago ostensibly so that I would not discover gifts he purchased for me online. Everything was password protected, so I had no idea what he was sending or to whom. This receipt was for a site called, Silver Daddies. Oh, dear God, not more beard products. The man uses more beard grooming products than Rip van Winkle. What did he order now? I clicked. There were naked men in all sorts of suggestive poses with introductions. My breakfast was back in my mouth. This was obviously some gay hook up site. Still, I trusted. Maybe this was a subscription for Rick. He was always giving him gifts. I said nothing, though he claims we had discussed it. My memory is not clouded by vodka, and I have zero recollection of that conversation. I only know that the receipt had been removed from the sent folder by the next day.

Two weeks later came the bombshell. He had left his Facebook account up and open on the computer. I was not overtly snooping, but this was too tempting, and I had become too suspicious. It was early morning when I normally checked email, and he prepared (Two whole hours of prep!) to go to work. Our younger son was working out in the basement, so I was alone in the office. I clicked. There it was in black and white, a conversation with Mick. It was something like this…

…I truly hate being married. You know that I consider you my first love. Had we stayed together; you would not be HIV positive. We could be two old college professors, living a good life together.

Suddenly, 2 + 2 no longer equaled five. I had my answer. I was married to a gay man. There was no doubt about that. As I confronted him with my discovery, our son walked up from the basement and stood behind his father. He heard it all, from my accusation to his father's last words, "I will call an attorney." For the first time in my 63 years, someone allowed me to cry on a shoulder, and that shoulder belonged to my son.

Mick is still a bit of a mystery. I know that he is even older than I. I believe that he was a student at the college, which housed the seminary. They met there. They had their tryst there, but I do not think he was a seminarian there.

Mick had served in Viet Nam, and I believe was going to school on the GI bill. He did try a vocation at several other Catholic seminaries, without success. He became an Episcopalian because of the Catholic stance on gays and lesbians. He is now an ordained Dominican in that denomination and an adjunct psychology professor.

Rick turned out to be the lover of the Franciscan priest's gay roommate, a roommate, who should not have been. I suspect he was present when the group of prospective seminarians met for dinners and sleepovers. Rick never had a vocation to the priesthood. I honestly do not think that he was ever even interested in my ex-husband, but my ex was certainly interested in him.

I was the one and only female sexual partner in his life. He now says that he wished we had consummated our relationship prior to marriage because he would have realized how unsatisfying sex with a woman is for him. Gee, thanks.

He told me that he thought he was bi when we married. I asked why he never mentioned it. Of course, this was my fault. I never asked. Why would I ask something like that? I never thought of it. He pursued me. I doubt he would have been honest. He is a consummate liar. He has a talent. He can repeat lies and never change a detail. Altering details is how most liars are caught, but not him. He is gifted.

As it turns out, he had been planning to divorce me for some time. I opened his closet door and ran out. He has stayed inside and slammed the door shut. Only people, who have talked to me, know the truth. His family and his few straight friends have all been told that our marriage dissolved because I am controlling, domineering, and would not allow him to have friends. I have been removed from his family tree. He never takes responsibility for anything. He never lost a job because of his performance or actions, and I bought all the convoluted reasons. Now the break-up of his marriage is the result of my actions. Was I perfect? Of course not, but I did nothing that required a visit to an attorney. If you know me, you also know that I am neither controlling nor domineering. I learned to be a people pleaser as a child. I would not allow him to have friends?!? My mere existence precluded him from having the friends he wanted, boyfriends, lovers. He did not want the responsibility of a family. He told our younger son that he likes the three of as human beings; he just does not like living with us. As far as he is concerned, his sexual identity is not an issue.

The divorce was finalized in November of 2018. I would not call it painless, but it is finished. We have not spoken since then. I have no strings tied to him at all, other than our kids. I have good relationships with both of my sons, their girlfriends, and the girlfriends' families. Our sons have established themselves in careers and are productive members of society. The older is a Naval officer, and the younger is a police officer with a freshly minted MS in Criminal Justice. Yes, I raised them well. He helped at the start, but I did most of the hard work, so I will take the credit. I know that there will be weddings and grandchildren in the future, and I will deal with my ex-husband as needed. I hold my head up high because I know that I did not cause this. I was a good wife and mother. I did nothing to deserve this. I have survived, and I am determined to thrive.

Tess' Story

I was born in 1958 in London, the eldest of four, to Christian parents. I had a privileged, happy childhood. Although strict in some ways, it was very free in others. I always felt safe at home and knew I was loved. We had amazing holidays, touring Europe for a month every summer. We had a motor boat and spent a lot of time messing about on rivers or the sea - a good antidote to city life. My mum and dad were both strong characters and very much a team. So I had good role models. They were not pushy about their sexuality, but neither were they prudish. As children we had seen them in the bath or getting dressed or mum breast feeding my younger siblings, all of which they were quite relaxed about. When I was about 10, I went downstairs one night and caught them making love in front of the fire. My dad looked up and said, "Go away, you're interrupting," so I did!

My parents bought a second home in 1978 and moved the following year with my two younger sisters, later selling the London house. By this time I was working and had moved out into a local flat (apartment) shared with three girlfriends. I had a couple of long-term relationships with men in my teens and early twenties. In 1981, bored with administrative jobs that didn't challenge me, I went to University in Sheffield.

In Sheffield I rekindled my Christian faith which had slipped, after discovering sex and having lovely, but non-Christian boyfriends. Here, I met Dan. We got on very well and were just friends but both loathed the halls of residence. So we moved into a student flat with another

Christian man. One evening, after Dan and the other guy had an argument, he asked me to go for a walk with him because he needed to vent. We dealt with that and were on top of a hill overlooking the city. God was speaking to him (non-Christians probably won't get that) and prompted Dan to ask me to marry him. Much to my surprise, I felt sure this was right before God, and I said yes!

At the time, I was not interested in another relationship as I was sore following a break up. So this was a bit of a shock! We'd got engaged, without even going out! We were very close and loved each other as friends and understood each other, but at that point there had never been any hint of physical contact between us. Dan then moved out of the flat, because as Christians we knew we needed to refrain from 'the appearance of evil' - although we we're aware we were not having sex; others weren't so the gospel could be brought into disrepute unless we lived separately. So a girlfriend moved into the flat, and Dan moved in with a couple in our church for a few months.

We became physical in as much as there was plenty of kissing and cuddling (with clothes on) - everything seemed normal, no reason to suppose there would be a problem later on. I completely fell in love.

During our engagement, he had to go on a work placement a couple of hundred miles away as part of his course. One time when he came to visit, he said he wasn't sure about going ahead with the wedding. He wasn't sure if he loved me. My response was to get on my knees and pray. I was of course emotional, very upset, but fundamentally I trusted God and was sure He would bring good out of this unforeseen situation. I was confident that God would bring me through, whatever happened. I thought Dan was just getting 'cold feet' - lots of people get wedding nerves. We talked about delaying but neither of us wanted to. With hindsight, I wonder if it was because he had an inkling he fancied men.

There were already problems with my parents, who liked Dan, but we had inadvertently stirred up a hornet's nest of unresolved angst from their own wedding, and their behaviour was out of character. So I was also dealing with the painful fall-out from that, as my usually predictable family plunged into crisis almost causing the wedding to be called off.

We got through that and were married at end of our first year at university. On our wedding night he was a virgin, but I wasn't. I was looking forward so much to making love... but he looked at me in my lovely lingerie and said I was bigger than he thought and he was too tired. He rolled over and went to sleep. I was devastated.

His sister (probably the only girl he'd seen wearing underwear up to that point) had an eating disorder. She had a very athletic, boyish figure and was underweight. In contrast, I was slim at 5 feet 8 inch and 9.5 stone, barely a size 12 (American size 8), with an hour-glass figure. I'd never been short of interest from men and was completely floored by his response and so upset, lying in bed beside him, trying to make sense if it, while he slept. The following morning we showered together and made love. He later said his refusal to have sex on our wedding night was because he was 'naive'- but I felt that reflected a lack of interest.

After our honeymoon we moved into a rented house for a year before we lived in community house for two years with another couple forming deep friendships and aiming to live 'sharing everything in common' as the early apostles had done. We had a top floor bed sit in a shared house, the other couple had a bedroom and private lounge so there was opportunity for privacy as well as sharing. His libido did not seem to be as high as mine, but was definitely there and we got on with our life.

The next inkling that something was "off" came whilst living in this community house. We went on a marriage course organised by our church. During this time each participant had some private counselling and in coming back together afterwards, he revealed that he had wondered aloud to the counsellors whether he might be homosexual. The counsellors (a man and woman, but neither were professionally qualified in psychological counselling) had dismissed this idea. In hindsight I can see this was a seriously misguided thing to do and also damaging, because he then did dismiss it for several more years. Hence 'the gay thing' (TGT) remained 'under the radar' as he sought to take his responsibilities as a husband seriously and get on with married life. We were very happy other than the mismatched sexual appetites; we were good friends.

We finished our degrees, moved south to the outskirts of London with work, and bought our first house nine months later. We were involved in a local church, took faith seriously, and expected God to move in 'signs and wonders,' inspired by the visit of John Wimber (founder of Vineyard movement) to Wembley in 1985. We both changed jobs a couple of times, climbing the career ladder, which brought new challenges that we faced together. They were happy days!

God called Dan to study theology, and he was offered a place to do a degree in London. By this time we were worshipping in a Charismatic Anglican Church which had also been impacted by the Vineyard movement. College was on the opposite side of London, a two hour commute and during that first year we lived in seven places! This was not sustainable, so I got a new well-paid job to keep us both afloat, and we moved into rented accommodation nearby whilst letting out our house to cover the mortgage. In a summer seminar at the end of that academic year, Dan had an epiphany. He recognized he has same sex attraction (SSA). He offered me a divorce and commenced support with a Christian charity Courage Trust, affiliated to Exodus International. At the time Leanne Payne was acknowledged as an expert - the groups' aim is to promote healthy relating among gay Christians. We attended counselling together.

This revelation was an enormous blow, but made sense of the forgotten incident from several years previously on the marriage course of our wedding night. I deeply loved both Dan and God, and felt confident that there was nothing we couldn't face together as we had been in the habit of doing, and that. "God could fix this; nothing is too big for Him." We believe that "God could fix this, nothing was too big for Him". This was not mere naivety, and I still believe it, but things did not turn out as I had at that time hoped they would. The following year, continuing to struggle with his sexuality, Dan made his first suicide attempt by overdosing. He was clearly deeply traumatized by the internal struggle he was going through, believing that the practice of homosexuality is sinful, yet struggling with attraction to men.

God called us together into ministry (prophetically) in the Anglican Church (for US readers, think Episcopalian). Dan applied, made it through the selection process, and was accepted. Two years of Ministry training at another London College ensued. This was close to where I had grown up, so the area was familiar and long-term friends were around me. We attended a Charismatic Anglican Church, which also had links with the Vineyard movement, as did our church in Sheffield where we had been married and regularly went back to visit friends. A pastor who had worked with John Wimber for many years visited and prophesied over Dan identifying correctly the first parish in which he would be the curate. I continued working and at the beginning of the second year we had our first daughter. It was a difficult pregnancy; I had a pre-eclampsia and ended up needing four months off work with multiple hospital stays prior to the delivery, as medical staff tried to control the symptoms. Further postnatal trauma continued for three months afterward. Dan had always wanted children and was a devoted and hands-on dad.

We moved north of London to begin his first ministerial post as a curate. In 1994 our second daughter was born in a traumatic delivery. I did not return to work after the birth. We had two children under17 months and since moving north of London, would have faced a two hour commute.

In 1994 we sensed God calling us to 'get into the river,' in a prophetic word about Niagara. It was the time of the 'Toronto blessing' - signs and wonders centered on the Airport Vineyard church which drew Christians from all over the world. Obedient to that call, we went over there with a baby and toddler in tow. Dan was having a huge inner struggle. I was blessed by the ministry but ultimately disappointed as I had been praying Dan could resolve TGT

(I was praying for his healing). Dan in contrast hardened; perhaps his struggle was crystallizing in that environment. He seemed uncharacteristically withdrawn, and he appeared to be angry chose not to go forward for prayer. At this point I believed that a homosexual orientation was something wrong (like faulty wiring) from which a person could be 'fixed.' I don't have that perspective any longer, although I do believe God can and does heal. And there are some people for whom this has happened, but as far as I can understand, just a small minority. For most, like Dan, the reality of same-sex attraction sets up a conflict with evangelical persuasion, and most struggle to resolve that. They may move away from faith altogether or adopt a more liberal perspective.

Shortly before her second birthday, our younger daughter was diagnosed with Cerebral Palsy. I never asked in the face of this, "Why us?" Both Dan and I took the stance, "Why not us?" CP affects 1 in 400 children, and our child had the benefit of two loving parents who would stand up, love, and advocate for her. This precipitated a massive (pre-internet) learning curve, private's consultations, physiotherapy (physical therapy for US readers!), and special needs education.

With an older child in nursery (kindergarten), the logistics were awful. I spent most of my time driving kids around, but we shared the car! Our older daughter was developing precociously, it was clear from a young age she was very bright and had leadership skills. So I was trying to deal with very different needs of my two children, and the gay thing, whilst running a home that everybody in the church felt entitled to have a piece of because my husband worked from home! Later the older one had to be schooled out of area as logistics got worse, so we were dealing with

3 education authorities for 2 kids under 5! I was doing a 90-mile-a-day school run to facilitate their different needs in different counties. At the time there were significant pressures and some very difficult pastoral challenges in the church. We sold our house (which had been let out) in a falling market and used equity to cover special needs school fees. We were living as a family of four on £800 (Approximately $1000 US dollars). So there was no wiggle room in the budget whatsoever.

Inevitably, things came to a head. In 1998 Dan burned out, had a crisis of faith, and of identity. He resigned. His self-image was wounded from childhood bullying, and he had a rhinoplasty to change his appearance. Also (although I didn't know it at the time) he had a homosexual affair with one of the Courage Trust guys.

The diocese apologised for lack of support. The person who was supposed to be giving it was writing up his PhD and only phoned once in 18 months. They came to an arrangement with a neighbouring diocese that provided a church house local to the special needs school at a low rent. Dan was given a car (real provision!) and started work as diocesan communications officer. He did a foundation art course part-time whilst working there part-time, to prepare for alternative future employment. We attended the local church which was what Dan needed (no demands on him at all), and my oldest daughter became a child member of their robed choir. I really struggled – (it was not my preferred style of churchmanship) but wanted the family to worship together.

Inspired by the skill of pediatric OTs at the special needs school, I investigated re-training as an occupational therapist and discovered I needed 'evidence of recent study' - despite having a degree and successful career! So I went to evening class to prove I still had two brain cells to rub together. I applied to the three universities closest to us, which offered training. I had offers from all of them but picked the easiest commute. We also commenced a medico-legal case against the hospital where our younger daughter was born. They fairly quickly admitted negligence. However the case would run for nine years generating boxes of evidence requiring much emotional effort and input.

Between 2001 to 2002 Dan left the church and began earning his living as a graphic designer in a secular context. A year later he was headhunted into a different job, but the economic climate had taken a downturn. Companies were culling their advertising budgets, and six months in he was made redundant.

It was summer 2002. I had just graduated, and house prices were rising dramatically. We had spent large chunks of the equity from our house on special needs school fees, so we only had a 10% deposit available to buy a home. Until I had secured an OT job, we couldn't get a mortgage. We were starting again in our 40's. Although very stressful, Dan and I both managed to secure decent jobs and moved into another home nearby. Combining work, the gay thing, (which I referred to as 'the elephant in the room') and parenting with special needs in the mix, it was a challenge. Our younger daughter was seeing 12 different clinical specialties, and I worked out I was taking half my annual leave just taking her to appointments. And I wasn't even doing them all; Dan covered about 30%. I was also applying for benefits, supporting other parents of disabled kids and was a parent rep on the school board.

Our younger daughter had moved into a mainstream school and was badly bullied. She started self-harming (aged 10), so we got an emergency referral to Child & Adolescent mental health services. I do not know if there is a link, but like her dad, her self-esteem had taken a hefty battering from childhood trauma. I worried about history repeating itself, as it had taken me years to stop looking over my shoulder half-expecting something else after Dan's overdose years before.

Dan, having rebuilt his faith from the bottom up, we started attending a Charismatic Anglican Church in nearby Oxford which blessed us all. However, he continued to struggle with same sex attraction. I attended a support course run at church for people who had been sexually wounded. By this time our sex life was very sporadic and I found myself envying my parents who were in their 70s but still clearly enjoying that aspect of their life a lot more than we were!

Four years after our daughter's self-harm incident, Dan's internal struggle led to his second suicide attempt. This was another massive trauma for me, attempting to shield the girls from what was going on. Again I managed to get him to the hospital in time to save his life. A GP (MD) friend rushed down from Sheffield, joined me at the hospital, and took him back home where he and his wife planned to look after him, except Dan's dad died the following day. So he went to be with his mum while I 'held the fort' at home until the funeral.

We ultimately had to give up the medico-legal case despite admission of negligence because QC advice was that causation would be difficult to prove. We were legal-aided and could not afford to proceed privately.

Both of us suffered from bad sleep (I'd had chronic insomnia since pregnancy) and in 2007 Dan moved out of our bedroom and began sleeping in the study. At first he felt guilty (to be fair, we both needed sleep!) and would come up each morning to pray together, but this tailed off as he became more isolated and spent more time on his own, often going to bed early, disappearing at 8.30pm leaving me to sort the kids out.

In February 2008, Dan and I had our first holiday without the girls (who were looked after by his mum) while we went to Northumbria. By this time we were exhausted, and although I didn't know it then, this would be the last time we would be intimate. He was finding the SSA issues continuing to cause him difficulty. God told him to confess to me and the vicar that he'd had the gay affair 10 years previously. I was devastated! He was becoming more withdrawn and distant. Our older daughter noticed we were not getting along too well. I could sense this might not end well and started seeing a counsellor to address the issue of his withdrawal/depression plus my feeling we were housemates who were co-parenting rather than loving partners. This also included my feelings around the sexual rejection.

Dan had an increasing sense of calling back into ministry, and still ordained, he approached the bishop about 'permission to officiate' in the diocese which was granted. He commenced assisting the Hospital chaplain at our local hospital, who trained him up in a volunteer capacity. Later he left his secular job to work full time as a chaplain. Whilst at the hospital, he began using his artistic and graphic skills with groups of patients. This was rapidly acknowledged to be helpful and the hospital deployed an OT assistant to work with him. His job became a kind of hybrid role, amalgamating his vocation (priest) & passion (art). Having carved out a niche for himself, he approached hospital management with a business case and they agreed to four days as a chaplain with two days funded study leave, so he could do a part time Master's Degree.

What I didn't realise at the time was this was his way out not just from chaplaincy work, but also from the marriage. He was strategically setting out a new career parallel with his old one. I think that people struggling with their sexuality are adept at keeping things hidden. Although I do not believe that Dan has a narcissistic personality, there were a few covert traits, as he shifted gears and planned his way out. They were subtle rejections and easily hidden from those not living close to him.

Two years later we left the Oxford church we were all settled in, mostly because the old church buildings were not wheelchair friendly, and both girls were going to youth groups in two places, which wasn't working for mum and dad! Our younger daughter had by this time had multi-level surgery and was discharged non-weight-bearing. So we all began worshipping locally at Vineyard.

In 2010 I discovered on the family computer a browsing history of gay porn and trail of attempts to hire cheap hotel rooms. It was clear he was looking for hook-ups. He also joined Match.com (men looking for men) using funds from our joint account and was being "winked at" by strangers which I found nauseating. When I discovered this I was beside myself, I had no frame of reference for this. I drove over to see our pastor to whom I poured out distress and incomprehension. I felt the need to dress up, this urge to be womanly, to look like a lady, almost as if he'd stripped me of my femininity in order to prove to myself I still had it.

This stuff really messes with your self-esteem... especially sexual self-esteem. Needless to say, I confronted him with my findings after praying with her. He was deeply apologetic and cancelled the dating site membership. Part of what I found difficult was that it could equally easily have been one of the girls who could have stumbled across his double life. It wasn't, but I was still horrified.

His masters course meant Dan had to have ongoing psychodynamic therapy himself plus formal supervision. These we had to pay for and it cost around £200 per month. So he could no longer afford to keep seeing his spiritual director, who had been keeping him on track with the Lord. He started to question his sexuality and faith with the secular counsellor encouraging him to be "rue to himself," and to give those feelings full expression. Around the same time, I'm pretty certain he had an emotional affair with a man at work. I never had proof, but he started behaving like a giddy teenager. In September of that year he stopped going to church and has not returned since.

I also commenced a Master's degree, part time over 3-5 years. Part of my motivation was that I craved affirmation. I certainly wasn't getting it from my marriage! During this period it became increasingly clear that I was being 'edited out' of his life, except where I was 'useful'. For example one summer, Dan held an art exhibition in Oxford. A lot of work went into planning this. His Mum had been staying with us, and he wanted her there on the opening night, but evidently wanted me out of the way thereafter. So he insisted that I take his mum home the following day, taking our youngest daughter with us, which freed him up to mingle with his artist/gay friends without the encumbrance of an inconvenient wife! However our older daughter, who could discuss art intelligently, was a willing, experienced waitress and came with a very personable boyfriend in tow, was an asset to the smooth running of the operation! Of course, I complied, but I felt manipulated. He had been withdrawing emotionally for several years.

In August 2011 we were talking in the study, he got irritated, saying I didn't understand and went for me, attempting to strangle me. I was terrified, unable to breathe properly or escape. Our oldest daughter and her boyfriend were in the house, but the study door was closed. He had never previously done anything violent; I was completely taken off guard. It took a few days for the marks to fade, but the trauma of it didn't fade. I thought hard about going to the police but eventually decided to inform my GP (MD) only. Dan was mortified that he was capable of this and presented me with an enormous bouquet of flowers the following day. However, later on when referring to the incident he minimised it as 'my mistake' or 'when I put my hands around your neck' - which worried me, because there was an element of denial to it.

In 2012 my mum became very ill, she'd had years of battling Sarcoidosis and was on 24-hour oxygen with late stage COPD and other lung and heart dysfunction. Dan told me on February 29th that he didn't want to be married anymore. I said I wanted him to be happy, so if remaining married made him unhappy then I didn't want him to feel trapped. But I wanted to stay together, I felt we were married before God and I took my vows seriously. Like St. Paul I had 'learned to be content' in our unsatisfactory situation. The next day he offered a huge apology and said he did want to stay. However, what was said couldn't be unsaid and he remained torn in opposite directions and very closed off, for the next few months. I felt impotent to influence what was going on in his head.

The following month he finally admitted on paper that he is gay. I recognise this is not the experience of every straight wife, so I am fortunate to have it clearly stated. I discovered by accident, but I actually think he wanted me to find it, even if subliminally, it was intentional on some level. I went into the study where the family computer was kept, and he had left a notebook open next to the computer. He kept notebooks, mostly to do with his Masters, for example notes about and reflections on people he was working with. I never read them - confidentiality is a very well ingrained habit when you are a clergy couple! But this day it was a personal diary. I think he wanted me to see it, so left it in an obvious place because he didn't know how to how else to convey the information. He was feeling better from a knee injury & a run of poor sleep and put this sense of well-being down to the resolution of inner conflict, writing that 'I'm gay' had slid into his mind that week and he somehow just accepted it without a struggle – without a fight, question, or doubt. So he reflected on that, concluding that it just meant he should stop fighting against the feelings, thoughts, and attractions and stop the questions, doubting and denying. He recognised he was no different except that he accepted who he was. And that, clearly, relaxed and reassured him. He then repeated it over and over, stating *'I'm gay'* nine times! Except for once when he acknowledged he was possibly bi - before qualifying that the strongest pull was definitely gay. He wrote that it was strange but a relief after all these years. The struggling was over for him.

Well, as you may imagine, that stirred up a lot of emotions in me, too! At last he had moved from denial, and 'same sex attraction' which he used to say 'comes and goes' (I think it only went when I enabled him to maintain

117

his sexual isolation) - to acknowledging to himself the truth that he had previously found so unpalatable. Although I was reeling, I realised the girls could equally easily have stumbled across this, left open so obviously. And they were not ready for such a revelation, I was sure of that. So I closed it and returned it to the bookshelf, although not before photocopying it, as I had just enough presence of mind to realise this may be useful in the future, should he revert to denial. I hid the copy away; it was too painful to look at often. Four years later, after a lot more 'water under the bridge, it was added to my solicitors divorce file.

My mum died in May. I wrote and delivered the eulogy at her packed funeral. That summer was extremely painful. We had booked time off work for our pearl anniversary in August but he chose to use it to move his mother into her new flat. I chose to use it to make an appointment with my solicitor. I was in bits.

By late summer Dan had decided to leave. In September he identified a rental property but prevaricated about moving in. He then came to an agreement with the landlady and for the whole of October was excited and on tenterhooks, packing up his stuff, but trying to maintain normality for our younger daughters' sake (the older one had gone to university the previous year). He was keeping up appearances, like saying grace at mealtimes, while I was dying inside because this was so NOT normal! And I found these the most painful weeks of my life!

He left on November 1st, initially for a 'break' to consider what to do. I thought if he needs a year to sort his head out, I don't want to throw away 30 years, so it was best to see how that went. He and his mum came back for

Christmas dinner. That was a very hard 10 hours playing 'happy families' again for the kids' sake.

Our younger daughter's behaviour following his departure was deplorable. It was a deeply unpleasant year. Defiant, oppositional, verbally abusive, hitting out at me, she even pulled a door off its hinges which was no mean feat with Cerebral Palsy! All were expressions of anger at the situation with dad leaving, but I was still there, so took the brunt of her emotions. She didn't do the same with him. I was 'safe' I guess, and he had already proved he could walk away.

The following spring, after we'd had several woeful attempts to talk things through, he said he didn't want reconciliation. He was so far ahead of the curve, compared to me. He had been covertly planning (probably for years) and separating was a relief to him. I, on the other hand, was heartbroken, devastated and quite unable to know, much less articulate my feelings or discuss the future in any meaningful way. He continued to pay maintenance for our younger daughter until the summer. When she went to university in September, we split the accommodation cost between us. We were already covering her older sister's university rent so this was a financial challenge.

Later that year I commenced divorce proceedings - a hard decision but I had biblical grounds (all three: abuse, abandonment and adultery). It felt like there was more integrity in me doing so. The bizarre thing in England is adultery doesn't count in law unless it happens with someone of the opposite sex! So I had to use the grounds of 'unreasonable behavior.'

I started writing a journal after Dan left and continued it for about 18 months. By that time I'd written 600,000 words, equivalent to three PhD's (but a lot less erudite!) I also kept a three good things list each night to help keep a balanced perspective since proven by Martin Seligman to be effective in building psychological resilience. Working kept my sanity. It was a reason to get up and keep putting one foot in front of the other.

I also spent a lot of time tying myself in theological knots trying to work out what happened to my half of our joint calling, when the trained and ordained half had walked away from me and from God. Eventually I concluded it doesn't change my calling, however the direction of it, and outworking of it, would need to change.

It wasn't 'the church' that kept me in the marriage at all. I stayed because I felt it was right and because I loved him. There isn't much to say about the church as an institution because he wasn't working FOR the church but for the National Health Service which employs chaplains for the last seven years he did ordained work. And the NHS wouldn't care at all whether he was gay - had they known, it would have been welcomed as fitting in their employee diversity strategy! Plus, they didn't know. It was only in 2012 that he finally admitted it to himself.

He said he told the bishop prior to our separation that it was a struggle he faced, but the bishop himself is pro-gay and even wrote a book in support of same sex relationships. So there would not have been any kickback from the diocese. And we were no longer worshipping in the Anglican Church by then anyway--we went to a Vineyard church. So the church response was non-existent, as it was a non-issue for them.

In September 2013 I went to a Straight Wives conference in Philadelphia. It was amazing! Affirming, supportive and among people who really understood, it gave me the conviction that I needed to write a book started there.

Dan started undermining me to the girls. Mostly I think because he was scared of losing them himself. I didn't respond by doing the same, but that was hard because they had a very one-sided view of what was going on. Part of the problem was I was shoved into his closet because he refused to tell them that he liked men. He said it was not why he left. Although he had another boyfriend not long afterwards, he also had a relationship with a woman. Cruelly, he made sure to tell me about the latter, unaware that I knew about the former from a mutual friend. I wanted us to tell the girls together, but he wouldn't. I then asked him to tell them himself, but he wouldn't. Eventually after nearly two years, I told the younger one. The older one by then had worked it out for herself and had a discussion with him. He told them he is bi. Perhaps he felt that would be more palatable an explanation. Personally, I doubt that, I think he just spent years in denial. But that sexual self-definition is up to him. Both the girls support him, and I support them doing that. He was always a good dad and they're millennials. We had brought them up not to discriminate against anyone. And I am immensely proud of them both.

I remained in the family home, paying the mortgage and all the bills. To make ends meet, in 2015 I took in a lodger. We were divorced on Saint Patrick's Day of 2016. I was informed by our eldest who heard from Dan, after my solicitor failed to tell me! With several false starts and a turgid post-Brexit market, it took a couple of years to sell the house. In September 2016, I went to a second Straight Wives conference in Washington. Again very affirming, I recommend them to any woman who feels she is drowning in the murky pool of having a gay husband!

In late 2016, my much loved mum-in-law (whom I had loved and remained close to all through the separation and divorce) had a fall, requiring hospitalisation and a respite stay. She picked up an infection and was seriously ill but declined to be readmitted to hospital, which would have saved her life. Dan told our daughters and her niece, to whom she was close, so they all made four hour journeys to say goodbye, but he didn't tell me, although I was half an hour away. I found out the day after she died. This was cruel and intentional...

In March 2017, I threw a one year divorce-ary afternoon tea for those girlfriends who had supported me through my traumatic five-year-journey. In November 2017, I graduated with my Master's Degree. By then I was part of the 'key leaders' team at my church and next embarked on a two year part-time leadership training course which the Vineyard movement runs and have now completed that. So I did end up having some informal theological training in the end and no doubt will put that to use in the future.

My dad died in 2019. Despite being informed, Dan did not acknowledge that or attend the funeral of the man who was his father-in-law for over 30 years. And this influenced our youngest daughter, who didn't attend her grandpa's funeral either. The older one, despite being in the middle of medicine finals, still made time to come and support the wider family, especially me, as I delivered his eulogy, for which I was deeply grateful.

Dan has done me immense damage, not just directly, but indirectly through undermining me with the girls. It still goes on eight years after he left. Christmases have been particularly hard to bear, but I can genuinely say I am through this now. I have forgiven him. It was a hard intentional process; it cost me in therapy fees, but it has been well worth it. I do not wish him ill--quite the reverse. I have reached the point where I can and do pray for him again. At his instigation, we no longer have any contact but that suits me too. I feel sad about the way things turned out, but would not wish ever to go back into a situation which I tolerated for too long. It took me several years after he left to fully appreciate that he had broken the marriage covenant years before by his sex refusal and other behaviours. I would encourage any Christian women in this situation who are feeling that they cannot leave to recognise that they are not trapped. They can initiate change, it is not their fault, rather they married under false pretenses. Where women unknowingly marry a gay or bisexual man (even where this is buried so deep the man does not initially recognise it himself), their entire marriage is predicated on a lie, and that lie being that their husband is straight. It suits many men to use us as 'cover' for a double life. That is partly why my whole approach to sexuality has changed, and I strongly feel that people should be able to express themselves without being castigated for something they cannot change. I have not worked out the theology but the God I know is exemplified in the person of Jesus. And He was radical in his acceptance of those shunned by the society of the day. I think we who are Christians should follow that example.

In 2018 after selling the family home, I downsized, buying a new house which I was just able to afford. I am now mortgaged to the hilt in my 60's, but I am free! I felt at home straight away, and I have embarked on making it mine, with small improvements as funds allow. And I'm dating again! It took me 5 years before joining a dating site because I wanted to be fully healed without 'baggage' beforehand, then another year before I started meeting men. But I have met some interesting people along with the gropers and no-hopers! And I had one serious relationship. Although we are just good friends now, he restored my self-belief. It was so lovely to be desired as a woman! You forget what that is like, when navigating TGT.

What am I doing now? How do I reflect on my journey? Well I'm turning around the hard things to redeem them and help others. I am the County rep for an organisation which supports partners of clergy who have 'done the dirty' on them. I went on a weekend away with the group in autumn of 2019, and it was very life-affirming. This is linked with another organisation which campaigns for justice in cases of abuse within churches, and I did a presentation on clergy abuse featuring real life stories from five personal friends from church or missionary families, at a symposium in Cambridge in 2018, attended by three CofE bishops, academics, and others. It is sad that this was necessary, but it is working, the Anglican Church has just (September 2020) agreed to new safeguarding measures.

The experience with Dan has not put me off men or matrimony! I loved Dan deeply but he was unable to love me as I needed to be loved. So I am looking forward to the future, with my head held high and my faith intact. The coming out process for them (or the determination to hide behind a straight person) often shoves the bemused and agonising straight partner further into the closet than they are! I used the analogy that we went into the closet together, but while he was wrapped up, protected by the fur coats, I had fallen out the back into Narnia, frozen out in an alien landscape where it was always winter but never

Christmas! This experience is incredibly isolating. You feel like you are the only woman in the world whose husband systematically rejects you because you're a woman. I am collecting references for a book, which I hope will help other Christians caught up in mixed orientation marriages. I am supporting/validating others and trying to change the culture, engage with the church establishment, increase transparency, and raise awareness. My past does not need to determine my future!

Stories from My Website – We Too

In the early part of 2017, a movement swept the country called "ME TOO." It was a movement created by female actresses in Hollywood to bring attention to the widespread sexual abuse by producers and actors in order for them to get parts in movies and television. Women united together wanting justice for this atrocity.

In 2017, I introduced a new concept in my newsletter called "WE TOO." Here is what I wrote:

Many of us have been "shut up" as we are/were being "shut down" to protect our husbands' secrets of homosexuality. In this day and age, it keeps making less sense to me that we are standing in the darkened closets abandoned by our husbands who decided to find their "authentic lives"--but not without making us promise to "keep THEIR gay secret OUR secret." As crazy as that seems, it is the case for too many of our women. You might think that in the newest established world-heard "ME TOO" testimonials of women shouting their truths to bring public awareness to their horrific plight of sexual pressuring and exploitation, our chants would also be heard. We would be yelling at the top of our lungs, "We too!!" inspired by "Me too!!"

Nope. That's not what has happened--YET. Every blue moon we get to see an article, a YouTube video, or a blog that quietly mentions STRAIGHT WIVES. In fact, we are so excited to see something that touts our cause because so little ever makes its way to the media unless it is sensationalizing those few couples who have decided that sexuality really isn't an issue in their marriages. Yes, the media loves those stories even though it doesn't represent about 97% of us, misrepresenting our nightmares.

We are not lining the streets as activists do carrying signs talking about our plight. We're not making demands to be recognized as a group of women who have suffered words that aren't even part of the English language because those words combining our collective abuse have not even been thought of yet. And though I know you're probably tired of me bringing this up over and over again....well--I'm sorry. I have to. Not for me--but for you.

You see, I am free. I am free because for 35 years I've been "pitching our plight." Yes, since 1982 when I started my first in-person support group, I've been standing up and speaking out on behalf of straight wives. I took that chance and shouted out the unfairness of our situations on shows such as Oprah and Sally Jesse Raphael, and before most people even heard about straight/gay marriages. Since then I did my share of talk shows and documentaries for this country, Canada, and England to expose and educate the public to what we go through in our journeys of pain.

It was easy for me because I was a fighter for years before this battle. Fighting injustice in a meaningful way is what my life was about--even if it wasn't the conventional way. Maybe it's because I'm a Libra that everything in the world needs to be in balance. Maybe if I were born a month earlier or later it would have been different--I'll never know! But I didn't hesitate to ask people to support us in our plight to let gay men know that it is NOT okay to marry a straight woman, and even less okay to keep that secret from her while you're out there doing your gay sex thing.

Back then, the battle was more difficult. We didn't have the internet or the information that we have today. In the

1980's, people questioned me on how I could accuse such a "macho man" like my ex-husband of being gay. I didn't get mad at them because I questioned that myself. How could he be gay? He's a martial artist who could beat people with his hands. How could he be gay? We did have sex. How do gay men have sex with women? Impossible!! By the nature of the word "gay," it meant men wanting men--not men wanting women. I knew gay men. I had gay friends. I lived in California during the 1960's when gays were prominent and out there instead of hiding. I knew gay. I also was smart enough at the time of my marriage to my gay husband to know that you can't turn a gay man "straight."

I learned that lesson years before. In California in 1968, I met a guy when I was 17 and he was 23. When I found out that he was openly gay, I said to myself, "All he needs is the love of a good woman." Yes, that's how little we knew about homosexuality back then. I fell in "puppy love" with him, and he claimed he "loved" me, but that couldn't stop him from being gay. I was smart enough to say no when he suggested we get married. I knew that love was not enough to make a relationship work with a man who couldn't stop being himself--and he knew it too.

I also had a boyfriend named Andy in high school who came out many years later. It was a short run, but we enjoyed our time together. Gay was not a topic people talked about in the mid 1960's, so I was totally clueless not even knowing anyone who was gay. When Andy sought me out 10 years later, he revealed in our conversation he was gay. I had no idea how that happened to this strapping, good-looking man. I met him in Miami Beach, Florida for a weekend. The first thing I said to him was, "I am so, so sorry that you are gay." He asked me why. I told him that it was such a hard life for someone to live the 1970's. He said he was happy with his life, and please do not to feel "sorry" for him. But I did. I didn't understand how anyone could be happy living a life where they were scorned and ridiculed. But he had no intention of getting married to a woman, and he claimed that as much as he loves women as friends, it's **different** than loving them as wives.

So yes, I knew gay. Or so I thought I knew it. The equation was simple:

Gay = Same Sex Attractions

Not sex with the opposite sex. It could have never been within my spectrum of knowledge back then that a gay man would even want to have sex with a woman--and certainly not a marriage with her. How little we knew. How difficult to understand. How horrible to find out. How devastating to deal with--on so many levels.

I've been telling the stories in my newsletters for 18 years. Yes, this month marks 18 years of newsletters. 18 years of telling the stories the way they are as far as affecting people living in this confusion. 18 years of spreading the word to thousands here in the U.S., Canada, Mexico, South America, Europe, Australia, China, and Africa. 18 years of "thank you" letters for shedding light in a world that was otherwise dark. 18 years of validation of everything that I speak about from straight wives, gay husbands, parents, other family members, and best friends who were caught in this mire of confusion. None of us expected the gay "wrecking ball" that would one day roll through our path and strike us down like bowling pins in a lane.

This "straight wife phenomena" is not like any situation I've ever encountered in my long life. I've never seen any group of people who have been victims that are so afraid to tell their stories to anyone. I do understand--more than you know. I see the looks that people throw us when we tell them--looks of disbelief or that we are telling lies. They question how we couldn't know after years of marriage. They question how our husbands became gay if they weren't gay when they married us. And when the gay serial marriage criminals marry women again and again, how does that make us look? It makes us look like pathetic liars. So unlike other minorities who are willing to shout out about their horrors, we just get sucked deeper into that closet that our husband finally came out of. He bolted out, but you are still stuck in there--hiding.

He'll tell you that it is *not your secret to tell*. You don't have the right to announce he is gay to other people-- including **YOUR** support system. Besides, there were other problems in the marriage BESIDES gay. "**Hardee har har**" as Lippy the Lion used to say in his cartoon. Or as I tell people when they tell me jokes that aren't funny--*NOT VERY FUNNY*. Is your husband for real? There were other problems? Like what? You were suspicious of him while he was out there cheating on you? Like you would cry because he didn't want you near him and found you repulsive? Or maybe you didn't like the way he brought you home some sexually transmitted disease that he'll swear you gave to him and hold you accountable even though you never dreamed of cheating on him.

One thing I will say to you:

Living their lie with them is different than living their lie FOR them.

Once they leave, you are under no obligation at any point not to tell the people who are part of your support system. You lived **HIS LIE** with him for 10, 20, 30 or more years. Now it's time for you to start living **YOUR TRUTH**. You don't have to remain in his closet hiding when he is out living his "**authentic**" life.

And guess what? If your family and friends want to find fault with you for staying in the marriage as long as you did or leaving it when you did, they are not part of your support system. Avoid them as much as possible because you only need people who can lift you up--not put you down. You don't need your support network dictating to you about how long it's taking you to recover. This will take a long time--no matter what. Years of peeling away your self-esteem, chiseling into your feminine spirit, and questioning your sense of sanity through "gaylighting" will be a one step at a time recovery. Let's not forget how your life will have to be rearranged.

Rae's Story

My husband confessed before he died. My greatest shock was assimilating (it took me three years) his admission that he'd known for decades he had "a lot of the traits of a sociopath," along with 60 days of confessing the excruciating (for me) details of his double life lived alongside me for 19 years. But I'll save all that for another time. My eyes have been opened in the four years since he (a) murdered my soul and then (b) died.

Many of these men were already actively living double lives when they conned their wives into "straight" marriages. How could one human being do that to another? It's very easy when such a man is a sociopath and/or malignant Narcissist.

Lacking in or devoid of a conscience, empathy, and guilt, they believe they are entitled to exploit a woman as a spouse or life partner to receive the requisite tangible amenities - a second income, child bearing and child care, and numerous domestic services including errand running, cooking, cleaning, and laundry. All of these things have a monetary value. If that's what a woman means to such a man, the provision of financial enrichment and DOMESTIC SERVICES, such a man is, at best, stealing them, and at worst, ENSLAVING another human being without her knowledge and against her will to obtain such services.

It is the ultimate violation of another person's human rights.

A man's excuse could be, of course, that he didn't know he was gay. Really? That means in all his decades of life, from puberty on, he'd NEVER NOTICED he was attracted to another man. Isn't the essential determinant of sexual orientation being attracted to another person?

If a man is acting on that attraction without the knowledge and informed consent of his wife, he is literally playing Russian roulette with her health. He knows what he's doing but he does not care about the effects on his wife.

Or, in the extremely remote circumstance he was unaware he was gay, then his argument could be he was a victim himself, a victim of an intolerant society. Women have been victims of an intolerant society since the days of hunter-gatherers.

The "intolerant society" did not give him the right to coopt a woman's life, a life she could have spent either living alone without fear of being used or infected with debilitating or fatal diseases, or married to a heterosexual man who loved her as an entire human being.

In other words, she could have had the CHOICE to find her own happiness. She was deprived out of that choice because she was not offered informed consent.

Taking all of these things into consideration, in the event a man insists that he "loves his wife," that he has a conscience, and is truly remorseful for her years unknowingly bound to a gay man, there is a way he can prove he means it.

Yes, gentlemen, there is a way you can prove you are sorry. You should feel very relieved.

Such a man can calculate the financial value of all the "services" she provided over the years. (It was not a real marriage, remember, because she did not have informed consent.) He can then prove his sincerity by reimbursing her financially for all those services. If he does not have the resources to pay her hundreds of thousands of dollars all at once, he can amortize the total and pay her in installments.

If it takes 30 years, then he, in his sincere remorse, should do so willingly. After all, she may have spent 30 years of days providing those services. A remorseful person should be willing to make reparations without being asked to do so. Remorse without reparations is bullshit.

That's preposterous, you say. IT'S TOO MUCH TO ASK a man who wants to move forward and live an unfettered, happy life as a gay man to compromise his own happiness by diminishing his financial resources and security, his own life, liberty and pursuit of happiness. It's unfair to ask a man to give up his human rights!

Hmm. Notice any irony there? What if you throw into the bargain that he live the desolate celibacy that he enforced on her for decades, manipulating her with lame excuses instead of informed consent? How about decades of emotional isolation and heartbreak? He did that already, you say, while he was in the closet! THAT WAS A CHOICE HE MADE FOR HIMSELF. He did not have the right to make that choice for another human being.

If her celibate, loveless life of servitude wasn't so bad, then he should be willing to live that way himself. Right? Or at least reimburse her financially for it.

Or, in the alternative, he could just dispense with the fake remorse and sniveling about fear of social intolerance and admit that, for years, he could not bear to live alone within the rigid parameters of taking care of his own selfish needs. In other words, doing his own cooking, cleaning, etc., while he personally financed all the details of his life on one income.

He could admit to his wife and everyone else they know that he never was a victim at all. He could tell.them over and over until everyone who knew her understood that he had stripped her of all of her human rights because he never offered her informed consent.

He could publicly pass all that sympathy and understanding (i.e., the "atta boys" for having the great courage to live life openly going forward as a gay man) onto his wife. She could use some reinforcement as she tries to recover from the knowledge that a huge portion of her life was a sham and a scam. And she could use some financial assistance for the years of therapy it will take her recover from having lived in a mirage instead a marriage.

He could admit he was/is a selfish asshole.

<u>Debbie's Story</u>

Yesterday (Sunday) I received one of my daily quotes and it read… ***"To not have your suffering recognized is an almost unbearable form of violence." Andrei Lankov***

I read it three times before I could fully grasp the impact of those words. It made me want to grab a pen and write what I have to say today.

For 2 years and 7 months I have asked you repeatedly to acknowledge the hurt you caused me thru your lies, deceit, and denial. And yet, you have never once acknowledged the hurt you have caused me. Nor do I feel you care or ever will apologize. As I have said many times, our situation was never chosen by me. It was selfishly chosen for me by you. It wasn't anything I asked for.

Your choices broke my spirit; you left me bewildered, confused, hurt, and with an emptiness which for years I thought I would never heal from. You left emotional scars and an increased insecurity that I may never fully heal from. I try everyday as hard as I can to heal my scars which you created. They are deep, and I have a long road ahead. But, please be assured I am making progress, and I refuse to let your reckless choices defeat me.

You forced me as far into your closet as you were. You made me feel a level of distrust, insecurity, and shame that made my every moment a living hell. You tried to make me believe I was the crazy one. The person I married ceased to exist. When I married you I gave you my heart, my soul and my most precious gifts... my children.

In the last 10 days you have called me bitter, unforgiving and an antagonistic bitch. For the past 20 years, I functioned in your dysfunction and I refuse to be part of that anymore. I learned to lie for you to protect you. I hid from my friends and our friend, in order to mask my misery. My self-worth turned to self-doubt and my self-esteem ceased to exist. And you have the nerve to question me about bitterness! I am not bitter, just hurt! Hurt, that the person who claimed to love me, the person who I trusted to love me, protect me, and comfort me could do none of those things!

I have lost friends in this minefield, but I have gained a sister from another mother. I know who my true friends are now. I not once asked for their sympathy or pity and I never asked them to choose sides. I was forced, however, to ask for help, something completely alien to me at any time in my life.

It was humiliating and humbling. Not until you began to discuss our personal situation and tell people that I framed you as gay did I ever say anything. I defended myself from your slander. I have learned a valuable lesson here and that is to be cautious who you trust--and I trust very few. How sad is that? Another repercussion of our situation.

As for my being bitter... no. Not anymore... just hurt! Let's tackle "unforgiving" for a second. In my support group, there is much discussion about whether it's possible to heal without forgiveness. Can we move on without forgiveness? I say yes! Do I forgive you? NEVER. I will never forgive you, and the reason is quite simple. You have solely put the blame on me for our situation and I have repeatedly told you I will never accept the blame, and that will never change. You keep asking me to forgive and forget and start over. You robbed me of 40 years our marriage was based on a lie, I mauled you, and you want to start over. With what? You told me a few weeks ago your mother would be upset with me because I was bitter and unforgiving. In view of the fact you have not once said you are to blame for ANYTHING then what am I to forgive? Again, you try to make me the villain here. And I respectfully decline.

I have spent a lot of time away this summer coming to terms with what I want in my life, and who I allow to be a part of my life. Old friends and new, I am starting fresh. I want to live in the present and forget the misery of the last 10 years and put it in the past. Before I left for New York, I threw all of my journals away. You put them at the curb last week. They are a constant negative reminder of years and years of pent up emotions, frustrations, and wrongs. I picked them up from time to time and read and re-read certain entries over and over. I cried each and every time for that which was lost or never existed in the first place. So by destroying them, I closed the final chapter on the past. Last session, our therapist told me I had to find and create my own happiness and I have spent my summer trying to do that. Am I happy....far from it! But, I am vigorously working hard to find my happiness.

I have rediscovered swimming, walking, exercising and tennis. All the things for years you told me were frivolous and a waste of time. I have discovered new interests and I plan to pursue them too. When I told you what the therapist said about finding my happiness, you made a sarcastic comment, well I guess that doesn't include me. I made no comment then, and I ignored the comment but it was definitely not forgotten. I will tell you today, right here, right now... there is one thing I am certain of, more certain than anything in the last 10 years, and that is I will never look to you for my happiness. You robbed me of 40 years. Who knows how much time is left. The therapist was 100% bang on... I will unapologetically make my own happiness in the future.

Pam's Story

The ultimate betrayal happened to me. My heart was shattered after 20 years of marriage with 4 children and 2 grandchildren after the great confession came--the confession that the man I married had an affair with a man. The actual words, "You know I'm gay," came three more times over the next few months.

It was a shock, and denial immediately set in. Finally the Denial started slowing unraveling as his guard was down & I was seeing the red flags I conveniently ignored. I couldn't deny the looks at male waiters, comments about men's appearances, the terrible gay jokes, how he commented about gay couples, and the pride he had for knowing that certain people (i.e John Travolta) were truly gay.

I was already walking around in shock before this time. I had found the male porn that he thought he had deleted on his computer and a stash of crazy porn in his closet. Things changed in the bedroom that regretfully soon became evident to satisfy his gay needs. Now, I understood why he had no real friends, steered clear of social media, was disconnected and isolated.

I painfully had to accept it was the covert narcissism that enabled him to live this false life for so long. It then took another year to get through the shock of it all and start the process to be unmarried & start healing from the trauma.

Painfully, I kept his secret to come out on his own terms but instead he went back in the closet and found another beard. After six months of deliberation, I wrote an unemotional email to both of them telling the truth that he was gay with the proof. Of course she's under his narcissism vortex already and dismissed that this could be possible. This also came with heartbreak of telling my children (aged 15, 19, 27) and helping them through the pain of discovering an ugly side to their father.

My biggest regret was not immediately speaking the truth. By telling our parents and children that he was gay and this was the real reason for divorcing him may have prevented another women from being hurt. Healing is nothing short of a roller coaster. I've conclude that for me I need to deal with the gay betrayal, narcissistic abuse, and being divorced separately with the hope it will bring the peace and courage in the end to restart.

Patricia's Story

I married in 1973; I was 23, my husband 28. I had never lived away from home. When we married we moved from the city to the country. At the beginning all seemed fine. I had my first baby a year after marriage. When we came home I got very ill I did not get any support from him at all. When my parents realized I was ill, they arrived and took baby and me home. After that I was very disappointed in him and myself. I was trying to be the perfect wife (whatever that was).

Baby number 2 arrived, and I was much wiser. The marriage at this point wasn't what I thought a marriage should be. We did have sex but quite honestly because I didn't get any support with kids or the household duties, I wasn't very interested. Six years later, I had my third baby. I wanted this baby and hoped it would be a girl and thank God it was.

He lost his job, and I went back to work and college. At this stage I knew he had been unfaithful. I presumed with a woman (now I wonder). My feelings for him as the years went on, he got very cranky (always cranky) but more so. In 2010 I finished work. I began I suppose to take more notice, the kids were reared and gone. In 2013 I found gay porn and a second mobile phone with sex messages from men.

To say I was shocked is an understatement. We had stopped sharing a room/bed for a couple of years before, my snoring! The first thing I thought was this is how he gets his kicks, not in a million years did I think he was gay. I didn't think gay men or women married!

I confronted him with the phone, etc., and he denied all and said he was "just curious." That I didn't believe but I still didn't think he acted on it. I continued to root and found another phone. I kept track of this phone and through the messages, I discovered he was bringing men to the house for sex. No point in confronting him as I knew he would deny and put it back on me. Every time I left the house I recorded everything that went on in the house. I got the recordings, now what was I going to do?

My daughter was expecting her first baby and my son was getting married, so I wasn't going to say or do anything until all that was over. (I lost 2 stone). He actually took a man to the house when my daughter's baby was 5 days old and I was with her. That was Dec 2014. After that I found it very hard to keep my mouth shut, but Christmas was coming.

I confronted him Christmas night 2014. He was all set to deny again except I told him enough for him to realize I knew. The tears started; all he was concerned about was the kids knowing. At this point I really didn't know what to do.

I saw a therapist (who told me he was gay), but I stayed with him. I reckoned he would probably understand more, and he did. He advised me to tell the kids and see my doctor before my next visit to him. I told the kids, and the hardest thing I have ever had to do. I said I had recordings but advised them against listening unless they had any doubt--none listened. They decided he would be told to leave and given 3 weeks to do so. I told him that the kids knew--tears again, but still denied. He said he was "bi"!

He left at the time given I think up to the very end he thought I would change my mind. He texted me to tell me he had cancer. I said I was sorry to hear that and did he want me to tell the kids, none of them had spoken to him.

He was then terminally ill and my daughter contacted him. The boys went to see him in hospital once. I never saw nor heard from him. My daughter was with him when he died. The therapist warned me about the effects after his death not to let him do more damage in death than he did in life.

So I had to keep focused where my daughter was concerned and keep quiet. He was her father, she saw him deteriorate, and that was hard for her. My eldest boy (man) was very angry with her, but I think in a family the eldest sees much more than the youngest (I know I did).

We got through the funeral. I had some of his ashes and went to the beach one day and dropped them in the sea, I felt absolutely nothing. If he had said to my daughter at the end will you tell your mother I'm sorry that would have made a huge difference to me, but I never even got that.

I discovered he had been sexually active with men for years. He also told me before he left that he had one experience before we married. I believe he knew he was gay (homosexuality was illegal in those days) and he needed the cover so he got his housekeeper and 3 kids. I also think he got away lightly dying less than 3 years after he left.

Sarah's Story

Before meeting J, I was told he was a guy's guy, that he won't "put up with any girl crap, so he's a hard one to nab." I was 24 when we started dating, he was 25. He had only had one girlfriend before me and I knew of only one other girl he went on a couple dates with, so I just figured his lack of dating experience was because he was just that picky.

At the time I think I looked at it as some sort of challenge. I had more than my share of dating experience. A few serious relationships and lots of forgettable dates. He was in med school. A little nerdy, but really cute, and a lot of fun. I had dated the wild, fun, bad guys. I was excited to date a good guy. He seemed like a real keeper.

We got very serious, very fast. We didn't kiss or do anything physical until six weeks into dating. What we lacked in passion, we made up for in conversation. We could talk and talk for hours. We shared the same interests, had the same likes and quirky opinions. I was used to dating guys that rushed to get things physical. As anxious as I was for J to make a move, I thought, "Finally! A true gentleman!"

Our first kiss and first sex happened at the same time. We were both very drunk. It was New Year's Eve. I was looking forward to this night because of course a kiss would happen on New Year's Eve! It HAD to! I was looking forward to what the night had to offer. It was sloppy and quick. Not something I would call passionate, but we got the job done. Next several times after that, sex was unsuccessful. He could not get an erection. He blamed it on nervousness and stress. After several attempts, we eventually had success. He was so happy he started laughing and was in tears. Going forward, I think we had a pretty normal sexual relationship while dating. Maybe not the passion-filled sex I was used to with prior boyfriends, but this was true love. We were making love, not having sex, so it was supposed to be different, right?

While dating, he did not have call waiting...and he also could not use the phone if he was on the internet, so I would get a busy signal if I called while he was on-line. I could not reach him for nearly a week because his phone was always busy. Late into the night. He was in med school, so I knew computer time was necessary, but he always made time for calls with me. This was very unusual.

Not long after, I was on his computer and the screen was pulled up where history was visible. I had no idea what he was up to when on the internet for hours at a time, but I was curious. I saw something about naked Asian men. He jumped over to the computer and turned it off. When I questioned it he laughed and said I was crazy. He said I must have seen it wrong. I did only get a quick glance. I figured he had to be right. I must've seen it wrong.

Sometime while dating he had gotten sick. He made a comment at one point at being so sick (which he was) that he didn't get aroused when looking at this website of women in their underwear... and since he didn't get aroused at that, that shows how sick he must've been. Hopping on his computer to check my email, I found he had a website pulled up of men in their underwear. I stopped to think... was it men in their underwear he was "too sick" to get into? Many times while dating, I felt he was way too good for me. I had this awful feeling that as soon as he REALLY got to know me, he would leave, so I would convince myself when finding these things that I really was paranoid and trying to sabotage my own relationship. So I would dismiss the voice in my head that kept saying, "Something isn't right."

One day at his house, I was playing around on his computer while he was outside mowing, and I found an email between him and a guy. I could not see the email he sent, but the response from the other guy spoke of how he was confused as well (about his sexuality). He said he was in to guys, but had a girlfriend he cared about and enjoyed messing around with, so he didn't know what he was. I confronted J about this and he turned white as a ghost. He said he went through a short period of time in college where he thought he might be attracted to guys, but that it passed. He kept saying that it is normal when living in a frat house when guys are all walking around naked, masturbating in shared dorm rooms... that it's hard not to get aroused when that's happening around you and it just got him confused, but he's absolutely certain he's straight. He was just an immature college kid with little sexual experience and overwhelmed by the sex-charged frat guys around him. We stopped seeing each other for about two weeks, then got back together. Isn't it normal to be confused during college? You hear all the time about people experimenting. He didn't act on any curiosities, so that has to say something.

At some point while engaged, I answered his phone and a guy asked for Joe. I said he had the wrong number. Worth noting, Joe is the name he used in email above and the name he used later down the line in gay chat rooms.

While engaged, my mom said a woman at work saw our picture on my mom's desk. Through conversation his name came up, come to find out this woman had worked with his mom. This woman said, "Does he have any brothers because I heard C's son is gay." I remember getting really mad at my mom when she told me this. What should have been yet another warning sign for me, I took as my mom trying to stir up drama and label J as she had so many other guys. My mom was often telling me so and so, and so and so is gay. I thought, "of course now she's saying my fiancé is gay!!" It was easier to get mad at her than think the love of my life might be gay.

Sex would continue to be an issue throughout our marriage. He almost always "needed help." He would frequently have difficulties getting an erection and keeping one. He would always blame it on stress...stress knowing that I was worried about it by over thinking what it meant and if it had anything to do with that "gay stuff."

A few months shy of our second anniversary, I surprised him and came home at lunch. I walked up behind him and he was looking at a picture of a guy and was chatting back and forth in a gay chat room. When confronted, he was visibly shaken. Very embarrassed. We had a heated discussion over it. Me begging him to please tell me if he's gay or to at the very least admit he's bisexual. He said he was neither. He insisted when he masturbates that it's always with thoughts of women. Said he doesn't know why he chats with gay guys. Said maybe because it's good for his ego? Said he knows it's sick, but maybe that's it. I searched his web history later. It showed hours and hours of gay chat rooms logged. I found a Logitech webcam hidden in the basement closet. He promised to stop. He said it was a stupid game he did by doing it. That it meant nothing. I didn't find anything again until 6+ months later. Worth noting...I had stopped looking. I was in denial and wanting so bad to believe him. I knew if my fears were confirmed, I would have to leave J, and I couldn't do that. I loved him so much and leaving him wasn't an option I was willing to consider. I don't remember if I accidentally happened upon this evidence or if I went looking for it, but the day before our embryos were to be transferred, I again found hours and hours of gay chat room evidence. We were deep into the IVF process, emotionally and financially, and the next day was go time. That was one of the hardest decisions I've ever had to make. Proceed with the children

I had been yearning for with the man I love or confront him and end it. I did not mention it and we proceeded with the embryo transfer.

Pregnant with twins, I was on strict bed rest starting around 16-18 weeks. He was home quite a bit during this time because he was studying for his boards. He spent nearly all his time at home downstairs on the computer. I would get hurt and angry and question this because I was stuck in a little room in bed 24 hours a day seven days a week. He would get frustrated at me for questioning him and would say he was taking these practice tests for the boards. The boards were coming up. That is true, but there is no doubt in my mind that much of the time spent down there was in those chat rooms.

Once the kids were born, I would continue to find evidence here and there of him being in the chat rooms, but I brought it up less and less because it only started fights and only made him angry at me for snooping. Desperate to keep our family intact, I started to try to convince myself that if all he's doing is messing around online, as long as he's not meeting anyone, we can make this work. It's crazy to me the things I tried to convince myself were normal or okay. They were anything but.

When the kids were three, I got onto our computer to find he had left his email open. Not his regular email, but one with the name "jorunner". It was filled with names/emails I didn't recognize. I opened up one and it was to a man. They were trying to figure out a meeting place. J mentioned he had been meeting someone (?) at a gym near his work. J came up and found me on the computer and flipped out. He pushed me away from the computer and quickly logged it out.

He admitted to meeting a man that was from out of town in a hotel room. When pressed he said he thinks it was a Drury Inn in (nearby town), but said he couldn't remember. He admitted only to jerking off together. He also said he was in conversation with a man who was married and asked me if I would consider swinging with them. He got very angry at me when I said no, pointing out that I had said at one point that I would be willing to be open to things to keep him happy, and don't I want him to be happy? He was pouting like a child, angry that I wouldn't consider it. A few days later he apologized over and over again. He said it was very cavalier of him to ask me to consider that. He downplayed the visit in hotel room with guy since they "only" jerked off. As for the potential meet up with new guy he was emailing...he said there was no intention to meet really. It was normal to have those discussions, but nothing ever happened. Again said he's not gay, not bisexual, but he gets off on seeing guys get off on him. He said his fantasies always involve me, not just him and another guy. He said he's never imagined being with a guy while intimate with me and he said he's very proud to say that.

Enter Collin about a year later. The kids were four. He initially said he met Collin at one of the casinos. We were at that time planning a family vacation to Branson. Collin lived near Branson. He said they got to talking about Branson and this guy offered to help get our family tickets to Silver Dollar City, Dixie Stampede, etc. I think we got one free ticket to Silver Dollar City. I can't remember, but he definitely wasn't much help there. But suddenly I was hearing Collin's name more and more.

This was before we had smart phones. They would spend lots of time messaging on Facebook. When it came time for our trip to Branson, J said he would feel really bad if we went to Branson and didn't see Collin. After all, he was so kind to try to help us out with tickets. I thought it was weird. I didn't know this guy. This was supposedly some guy that he chatted with at a casino and now we're having dinner with him? I of course questioned the oddness of it. J said he knew what I was thinking, but not to worry because Collin was married. We would have dinner with Collin and his wife. Dinner was fine, but unfortunately it didn't end there.

We got back to our room and J went right to his computer and was messaging Collin. We got in an argument over it. I said this is our family vacation. Why is he spending it messaging this guy... and we just saw him at dinner. J got angry and said it was his vacation too. He insisted I was being ridiculous and he was just going to leave for a while. If I was going to act like this, then he's just going to go meet Collin for a drink. They decided they were going to go out another night, since we were in Branson and who knows when we'd be back. J went out for the evening with Collin while I took the kids out on a wagon ride then to dinner. J got back late. J and Collin were together 3-1/2 to 4 years. We would make another visit to Branson during this time. Collin and his wife stayed in our home a couple times and us in theirs. They did fishing weekends together. Collin would always stay in our house when I went on my girls' weekends. I questioned the timing and J said he knew I wasn't a fan of Collins, so it just made sense that he timed his visits for when I was gone.

Their "friendship" caused many fights between us. J would get angry about my suspicions. He would say, "Aren't I allowed to have guy friends without you accusing me of hooking up with them?!" Collin invited J to go to Paris with him. This was a few months before our own trip to

Paris was scheduled to celebrate our 10 year anniversary. J said he told Collin no, because it would be wrong to go to Paris with Collin first, when we've had this special trip planned for so long. I was relieved to hear that and made a joke saying Collin and (his wife) won't be going on ANY vacations with us. This PISSED J off. I said it flippantly, not thinking it would ever even be a thing, but J got very angry. He questioned why it's not something that would be considered. I told him though (his wife) is very nice, I don't love Collin. I don't want him on our family vacations and frankly that's just weird. We continued to argue about this until we just dropped it.

Obviously we weren't going to agree on that. Other than Collin spending part of our Branson trips with us (hung at pool with us, went to Silver Dollar City with us, dinner), a vacation together didn't come up again. Fast forward to 2012, the kids were 8...we went to a wedding and J came home smashed. He passed out in the bed and started vomiting off the side of the bed. As I was cleaning it up, I noticed his phone. Normally his phone was always on him. Never had I had an opportunity to try and check it, though I had wanted to many times. He was out cold, so this was my chance. It was password protected. I had no idea what it could be, but magically got it right my second try. It was 7535. This was the last four digits of Collin's phone number. I didn't know that at the time, but I'm guessing it's a number I tried because it also happened to be the last four digits of J's phone number when we were dating. I clicked on Collin's name and immediately felt faint and like I could throw up. Right there was a link to a site Collin had sent to him. I can't remember the name or what it was, but it was clearly a gay website. I took his phone to another room and read their texts for hours. I was reading for hours and only got back as far as two weeks.

There was so much because they texted constantly. A fellow doctor from J's work made a comment to me at a social gathering that he's never seen anyone text anyone as much as J texted me. He laughed and told the people around us that J texts me throughout his whole shift (at work). He said we can't get enough of each other and laughed. I laughed along, but was immediately stung because J didn't text me from work. I knew it was Collin he was texting. The things I read on his phone broke me. They spoke of their sexual encounters. J had recently been in Branson to visit Collin and he was saying how hot their sex was last time he was there. He spoke of how wild it was and how he was turned on just thinking about it. He then went on in detail of this sexual encounter start to finish. There were pictures exchanged of their penises, their butt holes, pictures of themselves ejaculating. They told each other "I love you."

Collin mentioned seeing them as old men together someday. J said he thought of that too but he could never leave me. He told Collin he loved him, but loved me more. I contacted friends and made arrangements for the kids to be picked up first thing in the morning so I could confront him about this. I contacted my lawyer friend and told her I was leaving J and would need her help. We were supposed to host a birthday party for my grandma the next day, so I sent out emails saying I was sick and had to cancel. And I emailed Collin's wife to fill her in on all I had learned.

I got J out of bed sometime late morning, though I do believe he was still half drunk. I told him of what I had done, what I had read. He somehow didn't look surprised. He dryly said, "I f*cked up, didn't I?" I told him I was done. I told him I wanted a divorce (this wasn't the first time I had asked for one, but this is the first time he took me serious. In fact when asking for one before, he matter of factually told me, "Well you're not getting one." We never got further than that.). He pointed out I wasn't crying. He said I didn't even look upset. It's because I always knew. I always knew that this is how things would end. I would walk in on him with someone. Some man would call to tell me they were f*cking my husband. Or he would finally admit he's gay and leave. I loved him dearly, but I knew not to get too comfortable in our marriage. I always felt I was on borrowed time. He was never wholly mine. He finally saw I wasn't budging. I meant it. He had lied and lied for years and years, but he couldn't lie himself out of this one. I read it all in his own words on his phone. He broke down. He was sobbing and shaking and pounding the couch with his fists. He was sobbing and yelling that he hated himself, he'd f*cked everything up, he didn't deserve me, he deserved to die. He said he needed to kill himself. I was in a panic. I knew the right thing to do was call 911.

He was threatening to kill himself. I was scared and confused, not knowing what to do. He worked in the ER and had just started as medical director for several ambulatory districts. I knew if I called 911, he would be picked up by and delivered to his peers. The people he worked with every day. If me leaving him didn't kill him, that would. It was a big gamble not calling, but I didn't. I made a desperate call to our friend Paul, hoping he could come, but he was out of town at the time and was unable. I called his mom, but then he flipped out and told me to have her turn around. I stood firm for several days. He continued to beg and plead and promised to be the husband I deserved. He begged me not to break our family apart. He said it would destroy our kids, that his parents' divorce destroyed his. He promised no more secrets. He said he'd give me all his passwords....I could check any time. He said I can ask where and what he is doing as many times as I want and he promised to not get angry. He would always understand and spend the rest of his life making it up to me. I agreed to stay. I hated him at that time and for what he had put me through. The anger and guilt he pushed at me for questioning what was happening in my own home. But I stayed for the kids. I decided at that moment that my happiness didn't matter, but theirs certainly did. I also told him no more mess ups. I felt completely broken and I could not handle going through this again. I had given him more than his share of do-over's and I didn't have any left. One more slip up, and I'm gone. He said he totally understood. He looked filled with love and gratefulness and promised to be everything I needed him to be. Something happened though. I stayed for the kids, but found myself falling in love with him again. Things were really good. They were great...until they weren't. ***By the way, J met Collin on Craigslist, not at a casino. They came up with the casino story as a way to have Collin enter our lives as a new friend.

Things were pretty good I would say for a couple years. Not without incident. There was a gay "hook up" app he would frequent over the years called Grynder. I had learned at some point that he and Collin would argue over this app. Their relationship had some issues of trust as well. J was paranoid and worried Collin was cheating on him and they would argue over time spent on this app. Out of curiosity, I familiarized myself with this app. I knew what it looked like because I had even found J on it once while he was sitting in the car with our kids while I had run in the grocery store. This was during the Collin era. I coldly told him to please not look at that while the kids are in the car and didn't mention it again. I knew how it worked. The colors of the app when texting look inverted (black background and yellow and blue text bubbles). Twice our daughter had asked, "Dad, why are your text colors inverted?" I knew immediately what that meant he was doing, but he would get angry at me for even suggesting it and said he was on a work website and it just looked like that to her. I'd ask him to show me (after all, after Collin he said he would be an open book and ease my fears any way I needed without question). Both instances he fumbled, trying to find what he was looking for but said, "He must've closed out of it and couldn't find it." Another time I saw for myself he was on the app. I looked out the kitchen window and saw him sitting down below texting on it. I called him on it immediately and he said it was a "moment of weakness." He assured me it was an isolated incident. He hadn't been on it since "before," and it wouldn't happen again. Another time our son was behind J and saw something on his phone he shouldn't. My memory has failed me on exactly what it was. Something that said something about naked college football studs?? Our son asked why J was looking that up. J laughed and told him he had to of read it wrong. He would never look up anything like that. I immediately pulled J back to our room and questioned him on it. His reply? Again...a "moment of weakness."

Though he had these moments of weakness, the first couple years after Collin were pretty good. Then things seemed to go downhill again. J would argue this and say we had more good times than bad, but to me our good moments were just that...moments. We didn't fight, but we quite frankly interacted very little. Just asking a normal, "What are you doing?" or "Where are you going?" would set J off. He would accuse me of being paranoid. Sometimes I was suspicious, but most of the time my questioning was simply conversation. Any question of who he was texting or talking to and he would get really angry. I would get a lecture on how if this was going to work, I was going to have to trust him. His reactions though only made me more suspicious. Times where I might not have thought anything amiss, I was suddenly doubting his stories, solely due to his defensive response. Over the next four years he would get very angry at any questions that might hint at me questioning his fidelity, so I would try really hard to resist asking anything that might upset him. He didn't seem happy. I would ask him about this and ask how he was doing with his "urges". I would ask if he wanted to talk to me about any of them. He would assure me he had no urges and everything was "fine." Now that there was no computer to check and I just had to trust his phone was free of anything "bad" (because it once again never left his person...and I never did get his pass codes), all I really did have to do was trust. I had no other option.

His treatment of me continued to worsen. He had always been very critical and could be very condescending. He would correct what I was doing, how I was doing it. I would make a joke, and if he would acknowledge it at all, he would make a confused face and simply tell me that I wasn't funny. It got to the point that nearly everything I did was followed by a, "Why are you doing that??" It was very frustrating. I would go back and forth from sadness to anger. I would tell myself if I could just try my best to be as perfect as could be, maybe then he would be kinder. He'd have to be, because if I was doing everything right, that would make him happy, and he'd have to be nice. Except that didn't work. I somehow couldn't do anything right, no matter how hard I tried. If he lost something, it was my fault. I must've lost it. If something broke, he'd ask what I did because I must've broken it.

Not only was our everyday relationship suffering, our sex life was getting even worse. Aside from the few months following the exit of Collin, and our first year of dating, we lacked any sort of regularity for most of our marriage. And somehow it was always my fault. He would say he didn't initiate because it was always him that initiated, so it was up to me. This always baffled me. I can remember a handful of times he initiated, but the majority of the time...damn near close to all, it was me. Now if he wants to say me putting my hand or mouth on his penis and then him touching me back is him initiating, then sure, he initiated a lot. And it was usually work.

He would gently remind me he needed "help," and not to get weird about it. He would assure me it's normal and it's usually just because he's nervous about what's going on in my head...knowing I'm going to worry if he can't get or stay hard. These last two years we probably had sex maybe 4-5 times. I can't say for sure. I do know this past year we only had sex twice, and both times he acted like he was doing me a favor. He certainly was not into it. Sure we went through the motions, but I felt no passion on his end. I would bring it up from time to time, my concern over our lack of intimacy. He would say it's normal, he's tired, this is how most marriages are with kids at our age, maybe he's low on testosterone...and the good ole', "It's not just on me you know. You need to show me you want it." Quite frankly I'm tired of having to "show him I want it." The last time I went up to him and tried to take him to the bed for sex, he pulled away, rolled his eyes and said, "Not today." He truly looked disgusted. This was the middle of the day. He said he was tired and his belly was "weird." That's the last time I tried.

Trying to make that effort without going as far as putting my hand or mouth on his penis, I tried many times to scoot over and cuddle with him in bed as he watched TV or played on his phone. He always said it bothered him that I read in bed...and he would say "How could I make a move when you're over there on your phone or reading your book?" So I would scoot close. He never made a move though. I cannot remember a time in our married life that he rolled over to me and started kissing me or touching me. I always went to him.

This year things started coming to a head for me. I was so unhappy. I was quite certain he was doing something. I had no idea what...whether it was hooking up with someone or messing around on that app, but I was certain he was doing something. His little snippets of criticism he would dole out over the years morphed into something else altogether. He was downright mean at times. There was no way this man was happy. In a conversation with his mom earlier this year, she expressed concern. She told me he's different now. She had found him several times talking down to her and talking down to one of his sisters. She felt horribly guilty for talking to me about him like this. She said she felt like she was talking behind his back, which she didn't want to do, but said she was really concerned because to her, he just didn't seem happy. She said he couldn't be if he's acting like this. I poured my heart out to her quite a bit. I mentioned nothing of the infidelities, but I did tell her how distant he had been and how condescending he had been to not only me, but the kids as well - one of our sons in particular. He would call him stupid repeatedly. I would get angry and ask him not to use that word with him, but he would say, "He's acting stupid, so I can call him that if I want." This son has extreme self-esteem issues. He calls himself stupid quite often. The last thing he needs is his father affirming that.

By this summer, I was getting lower and lower. We went on a large family vacation. J is always the life of the party. He is very funny, very intelligent, and everyone loves him. We were in a group of people and he was laughing and being silly. Suddenly it was just the two of us in the room and his mood shifted. He started talking down to me immediately. I gritted my teeth and told him, "Just once I'd like you to be as nice to me as you are to everyone else." I turned and went to our room and cried. He was nicer for a while, as was the pattern. I would tell him how hurtful he was to me and he would be better, but it wouldn't last.

Towards the end of this summer I found an empty bottle of Viagra on his closet floor. I questioned him about it and he was furious. He said that it was from seven years ago and I need to stop questioning everything and will I ever learn to let things go...and he stormed out. I stood there pissed and suddenly determined. I stopped and prayed. I prayed so hard. I prayed that God would please help me. Either give me peace with our situation and help my heart and mind be free of doubt or show me. Show me what he's done. If he's being unfaithful again, please show me. Show me so I can know once and for all, because in that moment I decided that my happiness did matter. 20 years we've been together now. 20 years of heartache and lies and broken promises. There were many good moments in our time together, but sadly the heartache and pain outweighed the good for me. God started showing me in just days.

J had this coloring shampoo that covers gray. I questioned him about this months ago. I asked why he was using it because it clearly wasn't working, because his gray on his head was still just as gray. He said it's because he uses it on his chest hair. He said he doesn't like gray hairs poking out of his shirt. I pointed out that was weird because he trims those so short...and asked if he used it on his pubic hair...which would be weird since no one sees it (including me). He laughed and said no, of course not. Well within days of my prayer I actually got a nice long peek at that pubic hair of his. Bye bye gray. He most certainly was using it on his pubic hair. May seem minor and meaningless, but in that moment I knew. I knew I needed more than that though. I rifled through all his things. He knows I've done this before, so I knew I'd have a hard time finding anything (many years ago I found a bottle of Astroglide in a bag on the top shelf of his closet. He said he had it for lubrication for masturbation.)

By this time he was glued to his phone. No matter what was happening in the house he was transfixed to his phone. This had been going on for quite some time (and had on and off over the years), but the intensity of it increased quite a bit that month. We would be sitting watching television and he would spend the entirety of the show scrolling on his phone and typing from time to time. We could go two hours without saying a word to each other. I would be sitting three feet from him and there were times I had to say his name twice to get his attention. Every now and then he would get up and go to the back bathroom and he would be in there for up to 20 minutes or more. I would walk back there and listen. The blower was not on and it didn't smell after he was in there, so it wasn't tummy problems he was having. I would question him from time to time on what he was doing for so long on his phone. Sometimes he would get angry at me for me asking and sometimes he would say he was looking at Facebook, checking work emails or paying bills. I had in the past ask, "Are you on that app???" He would of course always say no. I knew the only way to know for sure was to get on it myself. So that's what I did. I made myself an account and waited. I found what I believed to be his profile, but there was no real way I could tell for sure...just yet. How it works though proved to be very handy. The first profile on your screen is your own. Then the other profiles shown are shown in order of proximity to you. So the profile next to your profile is who is closest to you and so on. The profile that was always next to mine when he was home seemed obvious, but I still needed to be sure. As he would drive away to work, his profile would move further and further away. And the real proof for me was when we went to a tractor pull about 45 minutes away. He went ahead of me and I watched his profile move away. I got there several hours later. I saw him staring at his phone, so I got on the app, and sure enough his profile was suddenly next to mine again. So I knew it was him. I decided right then I was done. I had decided this at many points in our marriage, but somehow I knew this was different. There was anger and sadness as there had been before, but what was different this time was a sense of relief and resolve. I had finally caught him. I had proof. I hadn't had proof in six years. I knew without proof, he would lie his way out as he always did; and there was no way he would grant me a divorce without it. Because without proof, I was just "crazy, paranoid and delusional."

Yet I still felt I needed more. He spent many hours away from the house. With his EMS job, it took him away all hours of the day and I rarely knew where he was. I wondered then if he was meeting anyone. I prayed and prayed again for something. Do I follow him? I knew that wasn't an option. I'm sure most of his travel was legit. I didn't have the time to follow him everywhere he went, trying to catch him meeting someone on the way home. But then something came to me. They make little tile trackers to put on key rings and stuff so they don't get lost. Can't I get some kind of tracker and put it in his car? So that's what I did. I put in on his car on a Sunday and the very next morning he went somewhere odd. I left very early in the morning to take the kids to practice. I remember seeing him still in bed asleep when I left. He looked to be sleeping anyway. Well he was in his car within 10 minutes of us leaving and he drove to a park about 15 minutes away. It's a huge park and he drove deep into it and parked in a remote parking lot that was back in the woods of this park. He was there roughly 15-20 minutes, then drove home. He was home before I made it back from practice. Well that didn't take long. I had the GPS on his car not even 24 hours and he already met someone? Odd thing happened after this "meeting." He wasn't on the app as much. He would pop in on it from time to time, but he wouldn't stay on it all day like he did before. I referred to this as his "moral vacation." I figured he got his fix...some guilt has probably set in and now he's going to "be good" for a bit. It would only last a couple days though before he would be back on the app full time again. The next weird outing was a little over a week later. He drove down the road to a nearby parking lot (popular spot for kids to learn how to ride a bike, learn how to drive, etc., because it's huge and usually vacant), he drove to one far corner, then the next, then back, then back to the other, then pulled out. Was he trying to find a spot to park concealed from others? Obviously he didn't find a good one and moved on. He continued driving to a parking garage about five minutes from there. He was parked in there for about 20 minutes then drove home. He again took a "moral vacation" from the app for a couple days.

I was so disgusted by this point. How long had he been meeting people? Thank God we weren't having sex because Lord only knows what STD I could catch. I knew I was going to ask him for a divorce, but the question was when. It all depended on the children. This was going to be hardest on them and it killed me that leaving him would crush them so hard, which I knew it would. They were just starting high school so I wanted to wait a bit. Let them get settled in. I didn't think they needed long, but I certainly wanted them to get a few weeks in first. I looked at the calendar. What other things do they have coming up? Two big things in the next month. I figured I could wait one more month. Tough things out to make the transition smoother for them.

But then he met one more. This time it was at someone's house. I was sitting on the laundry room floor folding laundry when he breathlessly says, "I need to go sign a 222. I'll be back." This wasn't unusual. It was normal for him to have to run to a fire station to sign a form or whatever. I took notice though how he was dressed. Athletic shorts and a T-shirt. I realize he was just running in to sign a form, but he had always seemed very conscious of what he wore when going on any kind of work call. I checked the GPS tracker and he was at a house and the nearest fire station was about 10 minutes away. I was so done. I knew then I couldn't wait one more month. I could not keep playing house, acting like I had no idea what he was really up to. It was time to tell him.

This may sound ridiculous, but I was worried about how and when to tell him. He reacted so strongly last time, threatening suicide, I needed to be careful. I didn't want to tell him before an ER shift or before an important meeting. I knew he would be very upset and I didn't want to drop that on him then send him to work. I had another fear hit me. This part of him is something he has hated about himself and worked so hard to hide for so long. Would he hurt me in desperation to keep his secret hidden? He had never physically abused me in all our time together, but people do crazy things when they panic. I knew his reaction six years ago was as dramatic as it was probably because he was still half tanked from the night before. I still had concerns. There was a news story that showed up in my newsfeed. It was the husband in Colorado whose wife and daughters turned up missing. It had come out that he had killed them. His gay lover came forward and said the wife had discovered he was having a gay affair and it resulted in the husband flipping out and killing them. On the outside they looked like a normal, happy family. This gave me chills. I didn't really think he would harm me or the kids, but my nerves were shot at this point and I figured I couldn't be too careful. We had an archaic gun up in his closet and what I thought were two shotguns, but upon closer inspection... probably just BB guns. I hid those. I bought myself a stun gun and some compact pepper spray. I thought maybe I could keep them in my pocket if things seemed to be getting heated. I had confided in one of my friends about what had been going on. I wrote out a list of wishes should anything happen to me. And at that point she had not told anything to her husband, but the night before I asked for the divorce, I had her give her husband a head's up what was happening the next day and to be "on call" if I felt I needed help (if J was threatening his life again).

Overall it went pretty smooth. Any fears I had of him losing it and harming me in any way quickly went away. He denied everything initially, as I expected. Until I told him what I knew and how I knew it. I told him I was on the app and could see when he was on it (little green light next to profile). I told him I had never messaged him on there but he did message me. Pretty recently actually. Days prior he messaged me and I panicked. I actually googled "typical chats on Grynder" so I would know how to talk. He sent me some pictures (they were older pictures because the wall color in our bathroom had been painted a different color several years ago). I asked what he was looking for. He responded, "jerk buddy." I asked if he did oral and he answered, "yes." He kept asking for more pictures and I got nervous and stopped. I told him I knew of his hookups and mentioned the three. He kept asking how I knew but I never told him of the tracker. I feared it would anger him. I think he thinks I followed him.

He asked if the park visit was me. I was confused. Apparently the first two parking excursions were just ways to get away from the house to sext on the app and masturbate, but the recent house visit, he said that was to meet someone. I asked what they did and he said, "oral." I asked if there had been any other meetings. He said there was a married guy he met. He said it was a weird situation where the wife knew. I asked where and he said at their house. I asked what they did and he said oral. I asked how many times and he said "he thinks maybe twice." I asked when this happened and he said that he thinks a year or two ago, but he can't remember. He assured me that was it. No more. Do I believe him? No. I absolutely think there's more, but at this point, it doesn't really matter. All I know is I can't do this anymore. This...all THIS CRAP has been breaking me down now for 20 years. We should have never married. I saw the signs then, but I loved him so much. I wanted to believe him. I chose to believe the lies. And lying is something he does very well. He can be incredibly convincing and come off as incredible sincere. And really, I don't doubt that he believes the things he says. He has found a way to compartmentalize these two parts of his life. His life with me and "that other stuff."

He said he's finally in a place where he can admit he's bi-sexual. I told him that's great, but he's gay. He adamantly denies this. And again, I think he truly believes that. I have a history of difficult and challenging sex that tells me different. Sex shouldn't be that hard. No pun intended. Gay or bisexual, doesn't matter. He could be totally straight with some odd habits, doesn't matter. I'm done. I do not want to be in this marriage any longer. I am 44 years old and have given my entire adult life to this man and I have hurt long enough. Through everything, I do still love him, just not in that way anymore. I would like to be his friend, but I have no interest being his wife anymore. And I will always be grateful for our beautiful children.

He's not going to make this easy though. He's been begging and pleading and making promises to change. He says that he knows he can be a good husband to me for the rest of our lives. He spent days pitching to me how good our lives could be. Even if I had a guarantee that he would be 100% faithful and honest from this point on, I would still want out. The cut is too deep. To stay would cause me more pain. There's a bitterness there that won't go away. I want no part of it anymore. I looked him straight in the eyes and told him, "I do not want to married to you anymore," but he won't hear me. He says he needs time. He needs 6 months to a year to prove to me he can be good. "Do it for the kids," he said. That's why I am still here after the hell he put me through. The kids.

I will not let him use them as a pawn in his game. I told him that I know once he finally "gets" that I'm not changing my mind, he's going to get nasty with me. He said he would never do that. I know better though. I'm reminded in little snippets he throws at me between the begging. "You know your life is going to be a lot different. It's going to change." "You know you're going to have to get a job." "You have to give me more time. When my parents got divorced my dad told us he didn't want this, that my mom was the one that wanted this, and I don't want to lie to the kids." I know he can be manipulative. I know he fights dirty when he gets mad. To move forward I'm going to have to stop worrying about his feelings and stop being nice. I wish he could see that how he handles this, how he treats me throughout this process, is going to determine the relationship we have when this is all over. I've given him years upon years of time. I'm not giving him any more. I've said that and more over and over again and he won't hear it. He gets agitated and says, "But it's not what I want." But it's no longer about him. It's always been about him. I had hopes that we could go through this amicably, but I don't think that's how it will go. I see me having to file and have him served. I pray this doesn't get ugly, but he does not like not getting his way.

* * *

In keeping with the thoughts on telling *our* truth, my recent newsletter from November 2020 explains to our women why it is so important to do this. I'd like to reprint this here since it is often a topic that so many of us struggle with.

Say His Name, Say His Name – Gay Husband

One of my readers asked me to address the issue of revealing her husband's homosexuality to other people when he specifically asked her not to do it. I think the majority of our women have been put in this most uncomfortable position of "keeping his secret." Do we owe this to our husbands? Is it really *our* secret to have to keep? I say **NO** with a resounding thunder. Why? Very simple. It's not our secret to keep.

I remember during my marriage how isolated I felt. Part of that isolation was because my ex-husband alienated so many people out of our lives--specifically MY friends and family. It was almost as if he could keep people away from me, I wouldn't "slip" and tell them the truth. Quite honestly, I was scared to tell anyone the truth because if my ex would have found out, I would have been vilified and punished. He was never physically abusive, but he was very emotionally abusive knowing how to attack every weak point in my ego and then some. He was also very volatile. As I've said before, he liked to "shout me down to shut me up." And he was quite successful at doing so.

So you may say, but after the marriage... well, after the marriage wasn't much better in the early years. He would be leading his gay life while warning me to keep "mum" so no one else would know it—except for the numerous men he was sleeping with. It was no secret to them for sure. And so I suffered in silence with people who were imagining where "I" went wrong in the marriage. To some he seemed like such a great guy—like many of our ex-husbands. They can charm a snake and convince people they are faultless for the breakup of the marriage. In fact, they are usually the victims. Why did they leave us? Because we weren't supportive enough or we didn't clean the house well enough. They usually never take the responsibility, do they? It's so much easier to shift the blame over to us especially when they explaining this to their families. And their families who looked at us as daughters now look at us through faulty vision based on the lies they are being told by our gay husbands. It's a no win situation. If we keep their secret, we come out losing.

In a world that now sympathizes with the brave gay husbands who have sacrificed their "authentic lives" to do the "right thing" by staying in their marriages until their families were grown up--while wasting years of their wives' sanity and sense of self-worth--I don't see any point in having to keep that secret any longer. Why is it our job to keep silent when they can live their authentic lives at our expense? That doesn't make sense.

Keeping his secret hurts one person—namely YOU. First of all, it puts you in a position of telling a lie on his behalf. That's the kind of lie that will eat your soul out and make you sick. In many cases, your husbands will deny that they are gay and claim that you are making it up to get back at them. I say **tell it anyway**. In time, almost all of these men will live the life they want to lead even if it's behind your back or when you're not looking. If they are gay, they are going to act on it. Maybe in the beginning it could be just looking at gay porn, but it time, it will be acting on those urges that won't go away. If you think your gay husband isn't having gay sex, well, then you are the one in a state of denial—not him.

I recently had a chat with one of our members the other day, and she insisted to me that her husband couldn't possibly be cheating on her because she knows where he is at all times. I explained to her that these men can be with you at all times and still be cheating on you. I know that as a fact because I have worked with several thousand gay men over the 35 years that I'm doing this. Their stories are unbelievable.

For instance, one man I personally know told me how he always went shopping with his wife to a local national chain department store. She would go into the ladies department; he would tell her he's trying on clothes in the men's department. He would exit to the men's department and meet up with someone in the dressing room (planned out ahead of the visit) and have one minute sex with the guy in the dressing room. This happened on multiple occasions.

Another man would tell me about his "dining experiences" in a large chain restaurant where he would go with his wife. She would be ordering dinner, and he would excuse himself to go outside to have a cigarette. He would meet up with a guy outside in the back of the restaurant, "relieve" himself, and go back to dinner as if nothing had happened.

One other man told me of his adventures in his HOUSE while his wife went shopping. He actually had men come over for what he described as a "quicky" in his marital bedroom and be done long before she came home.

These are true and validated stories. How does this happen? Easy. These guys have all kinds of apps to meet people for anonymous sex. They throw out the word that they are married men looking for fast fun—and they find it. And I know it works. A few years ago we had a healing weekend in Texas. We downloaded the app to try it out because we couldn't believe it. We put out the word that we were a "married man" looking for fun with another man. Within five minutes, there were six responses ready to come to the hotel—no questions asked.

Getting back to my original point, you can feel free to tell anyone you want the real truth. You don't need to keep a secret that is not yours to keep. Let people know the truth on why your marriage breaking up. It doesn't take "two to tango" when you have a gay husband—it only takes one— the gay husband. PERIOD. Well, not exactly. This will take me to my next topic!

How Many People
<u>Does It Take to Break Up A Marriage?</u>

Let's talk about marriage for a moment. Actually, let's first talk about straight marriages. Now I realize that most of my readers have a difficult time talking about this because they haven't experienced it—so let me be the one to tell you about it based on my own experience and the experiences of others that we know.

They say that 50% of marriages with straight couples end in divorce in this country. There are numerous reasons why this happens which include:

1. Marriage at a young age when you are unsure of who you are.

2. Marriage at a young age when you are unsure of what you want.

3. People aging and growing in different directions.

4. People getting tired of each other or just fall out of love.

5. Personality conflicts that develop more clearly.

6. Financial problems that break people apart.

7. Infidelity in a marriage.

8. Addiction.

All of this factors into the loss of a straight marriage. As I tell women I work with in this situation that there doesn't have to be a good partner and a bad partner—a marriage may not work with two good people just going in different directions. In every marriage there will be problems, but it doesn't have to come down to blame and stacking up who has more right and wrong points to justify the end of a marriage.

However, when it comes to being married to a gay man, all of this changes. It doesn't matter how young or how old you are when you get married. It doesn't matter what his personality is or what yours is. All that matters is one thing—he is a gay man and you are a straight woman. That is the recipe for disaster.

I hate when I first meet women who are internalizing what they did wrong in the marriage or what they could have done "better." I also understand why they feel this way. Their husbands have been training them for years to believe that his frustrations and their problems in the marriage were the result of her—not him. Women start analyzing what they could have done differently in the marriage. This is where I have to "knock some sense" into them to make them realize that nothing would have changed the end result.

Men tell me a whole list of excuses for the failure of the marriage—not of which, by the way, is the gay factor. They say:

1. We married too young – No, it's because you are gay.

2. We've grown apart – No, it's because you are gay.

3. My wife isn't supportive to me – No, it's because you are gay.

4. My wife isn't interested in sex – No, it's because you are gay AND you've done nothing to make her feel sexually wanted (I have to add that).

5. My wife is always depressed – Yes, because you are gay.

6. My wife is always suspicious – Yes, because you are cheating on her.

7. My wife is always accusing me of being unfaithful – Yes, because you are.

The list could go on indefinitely, but you get the point.

True, I became a different person from living with my gay husband. I was a strong and independent woman when I married him. How strong was I? In 1970 – 1979,I was the a local leader and later national director of a of an activist/militant Jewish organization fighting against neo-Nazis and Nazi War Criminals. I spent ten years getting arrested, jumping barricades, getting thrown down steps, hit by bottles—yes, I was strong. When I met my gay husband, I was charmed by his good looks, sense of humor, intelligence, and charisma. His strength drew me to him because I wanted a man I could lean on. I came to learn that his strength was that of a bully—always having to get his way or screaming and shouting. It didn't happen for a while. He didn't display any fits of anger prior to our marriage. After all, he was an excellent actor. He had been performing his whole life pretending to be a straight man.

We married much too soon. He was desperate for stability, and I believed whatever little faults I had noticed could be "cured" by the love and security he was so desperate for. I had come out of a previous bad marriage and was looking for someone to love. He came from an unstable family and suffered as a result of that. He sure knew how to get me to feel sorry for him. He had that vulnerable side that always sucked me in even after I escaped his mistreatment of me long after the marriage was over. I think these men target women like us who are caring and compassionate knowing that no matter what, we will still be there for them when the truth comes out.

We were only married for a short time—five years-- which produced two children. I suspected his homosexuality three years into the marriage, but by that time, I was pregnant with my second child and since he was adamant he wasn't gay, I let it go. He was not adamant that he wasn't bisexual. By year three, when he confessed to me that he had a "moment of weakness" with some younger guy, and after I went and vomited in the toilet for a number of days, I stated to him that I was willing to "bargain." Here were my terms: If you disappear once every six months and not let me know about it—and if you are with someone of legal age limit—I CAN LIVE WITH THAT. Silly me. Imagine bargaining with a gay man!! Well, at that time what I thought was a "bisexual" man.

Why bisexual? Because he was married to me. He had sex with me. Maybe it wasn't much and maybe it wasn't great, but it was still sex and that wasn't something a gay man couldn't do, right? Wrong. But no one was out there telling me that at the time long before technology had kicked in.

Did I change? Yes. I became suspicious every time he walked out the door wondering when that "once every six months" was going to be not realizing it would become more like once every six days. I would suspect the crime was being committed each time he left for any parts unknown. Was he always walking out to cheat on me? No—but I know that he was a lot of the time.

I began to recognize the signs. He would shave, dress up, wear cologne, and "look" like he was going out on a date—even when he was going to the "gym," the biggest pick up places for gay men. Yes, straight gyms. Steam baths with other "straight" men who had male indiscretions—but they weren't gay either. Gosh, I was so lost.

In 1980, there was no realistic information at all out

there even if you could find it. People believed that gay could be a choice you could make. I believed it. I believed that if I would try harder, clean better, lose weight, cook more, be more supportive, be less jealous (of nothing so he claimed), then maybe he could be a "better husband."

I was a prisoner running around the "circle of crazy." He was cheating on me regularly, but I didn't confirm this until after the marriage when he told it to me in a joking, bragging way. Yes, he had many a conquest of "quickies" in convenient places from the gym to our bedroom when I wasn't home. This man had no boundaries. If he gave me anything, it was the truth after the marriage was over. But not because I DESERVED IT, but because he thought he got away with something time and again. This is the sign of a true sociopath.

Getting back to my point, I did become a different person while living this nightmare. I didn't know who I was anymore and either did my family and friends. I had been isolated from them by my ex who made sure to have a fight with me every time someone was visiting us for fear I might tell one of them my suspicions about his secret. They just didn't want to come to see me anymore for fear of being caught in the crossfire.

I begged him to go to counseling with me, but he refused. He told me if I needed counseling, I could go—as long as I never discussed my "suspicions" with the counselor. If he found out that I did, he would leave and take the children. At that point, I was so beaten down. He had total control of all of our money. I rarely had more than a dollar in my wallet—another form of control.

It's funny. My ex fell madly in love with a younger man,

Billy, two years after we split up. I really believe he was truly enamored with this guy. It was different than all of his other hookups. He was obsessed. Billy stayed with him for a couple of years on and off. I had a number of interactions with him because the children would visit their father a couple of times a year. I found it so amazing that he treated Billy the same way he treated me. Not at first—but once he had him. This young man would commiserate with me about the way my ex treated him—the same way he treated me. Never believe these guys with personality disorders change even when they start leading their new "authentic lives." They don't. They can't. They don't want to.

Today, nearly 40 years later, things have changed. Women have access to information. The Internet is scattered with stories of women who have been married to gay men. I have had my website up for 20 years and had over 570,000 hits for information. Today when women want to learn about this disaster—it is out there. And yet, the truth is still so hard to believe. We still try to bargain with our realities. My heart aches each week when women contact me looking for some false hope that I can't give them. When women with "bisexual" husbands ask me if their husbands can truly be bisexual and just not cheat on them, what can I tell them? I tell them maybe it's possible, but in nearly 40 years, I haven't seen it happen yet. That's me—the voice of "doom and gloom" or rather honesty and tough love.

When I talk to women who lived with their gay husbands for 10, 20, 30, 40 and 50 plus years, my heart breaks for them. Living a life time of deceit and always wondering what you are doing wrong to create it is a painful way to live. Some women are beaten down like I was. They don't have the courage to take their lives back. I was lucky that my ex walked out in anger leaving me with two babies and $50.00. I had no car, no phone, and no self-esteem at that point. He thought he would teach me a lesson so that when he came home, I'd be so happy to have him back that I would give in to his (as my sister calls them) SHENANGANS. Ah, no such luck. In that one week I didn't weaken—I found my former inner strength. And as scared as I was to be broke with no job or minimal resources, I found the strength to say NO when he returned a week later. But being honest—if he would not have left for that week, who knows how long I would have stayed in that state of fear and hopelessness? Maybe I would have been one of those heartbreaking stories of suffering for another 20 years or more.

People tell me that I am one of the strongest women they know. Hardly. I am one of the *luckiest* women they know because my ex left me and after five years and gave me the chance to find myself again. I tell you my own story so you should never second guess yourself or blame yourself for staying longer than you should have. Never blame yourself for hoping against hope that your imagination was running away with you. Never beat yourself up for wondering why it took you so long to see the truth. We are good-hearted, loving women who try to find the best in the worst or at least the not-best situation. We need to stop blaming ourselves for any of the problems in our marriages. Any mistakes we made were directly due to the way we were treated and ripped down either passively or aggressively. We became different women than we were when we entered the marriage, and those traits that are husbands created were the ones that our husbands complained about. We were too "needy," "suspicious" or "jealous." I wonder why. We have nothing to feel ashamed about. No one has the right to judge us for how long we stayed or why we stayed. It's bad enough we lived through this experience. No apologies or explanations are ever needed to anyone—including yourself!

Final Thoughts

I started my journey back in 1982 after the demise of my own marriage to a gay man. We didn't have the advantage of the Internet in those days, so I was struggling through this with very little knowledge or support. Over the years, I have had the opportunity to personally touch the lives of over 150,000 women from all over the world who have contacted me for help. They have written to me to thank me for shining light on their darkness and confusion that these marriages are cloaked in.

It doesn't matter how many times I hear these horror stories—my heart breaks every single time. I try to talk and meet with as many women in person as possible because they need to hear it from me over and over that it is not their fault in any way whatsoever.

I still contend that almost all gay men who marry women do so with good intentions. They don't want to trick us—they want to fool themselves and Mother Nature. They are confused. They know they have same sex attractions, but they also know they want to be straight. If they can fall in love with a woman, have sex with her, have children with her, and be a family unit, they truly believe those nagging gay feelings will go away. But we all know they don't. They just intensify and become an obsession. I compare it to the toy called "Jack in the Box." You can shove that clown down in the box, but as soon as the song hits the part that says, "Pop goes the weasel," the clown jumps up. He can't stay down. These men push their desires deep in a box hoping against hope they will stay there, but in time they don't—they can't. The desires are so strong they take over all sensibilities. They start fantasizing, viewing gay porno. Then they start looking on line. What's the harm? It's just innocent fantasizing. Right? Wrong. Those fantasies become realities—and once the clown is out of the box, there is no pushing him down anymore.

Funny—meaningless hook-ups for our husbands still don't convince them that they are gay. They don't relate to the stereotypical gay prototype of men dressing up or acting like women. They aren't *that kind* of gay. They just have same sex attractions. After all, they are married with a wife. How could they be gay? That is how they are able to compartmentalize their lives. Some of them will never accept it, no matter how many men they have sex with.

Nothing saddens me more than having a woman come to me with false hope—which is what happens in almost all cases upon suspicion or discovery. So many of our women are told by their husbands when they are ready to leave that they have been "thinking about it, but haven't done anything yet." Or, "I've had one encounter but it didn't mean anything." I have the job of telling them that this isn't the truth. Over the years, I have worked with over 4,500 gay husbands who came to me for help. ALL OF THEM EXCEPT FOR ONE had previous experiences—and not just one—or two. The odds of these husbands not having gay sexual experience is none to nil. Some will say it happened when they were in college, but not since then. UNTRUE. Some will say that they have only watched gay porno but never tried it. UNTRUE. They've tried it—and they liked it—because they are GAY. Yes, I give no false hope.

Most of these men have been having sex with men for years and years with no regard to your sexual health.

That's why over 30% of the women who come to me have had to deal with some life crushing—and life taking—STD's. Now AIDS is controllable, but there was a time when it wasn't. I had women calling me crying hysterically that they and their gay husbands were dying leaving orphans behind. They broke me—literally. I would cry uncontrollably for hours for these women. And today even though women live with HIV, it's still a tremendous stigma that puts a damper on their lives, health, and future relationships.

Recovery is a process—and for most of us, a very long process. It doesn't happen in a month or a year. Some women take years to get past the grieving stage—and not because they want to stay there, but rather because the agony goes on—especially when there are children involved. In some cases, gay ex-husbands are very cruel. They don't want you, but they don't want to make your life any easier either. Some of them are downright sadistic to our women and never give them the validation they need and deserve. Not only have you invested 10, 15, 20, 30, or 40 years of loving and taking care of someone, but now you also have to give up your marital home and uproot your life because he will make sure that everything is POOF!!—gone. Your husband leaves, meets the lust of his life, and now you will have to pay AGAIN for this by being forced out of your home.

Many of our women lived in a state of confusion when they couldn't figure out why their "loving" husbands didn't want intimacy with them. In a few cases, the guys would take the blame and pretend it was their health—everything from low testosterone to diabetes. But most of them didn't have that decency. They preferred to blame US for their lack of sexual interest. I have seen the most beautiful model-type women learn to think that they were ugly and unattractive because their husbands made sure to directly blame THEM for their lack of sexual interest. They have been degraded in every possible way from being too fat to too flat. They have been told that everything from their breath to their body odor "stinks," turning off the men they love. And so sadly—our women buy into this after enough rejection. Can you imagine scrubbing your body daily hoping to get rid of an imaginary odor that you were accused of having? Some of our women know that feeling only too well.

Personally, I do blame all of these gay husbands for stealing—or rather KILLING—the feminine spirit that every woman is born with and should be thriving with in a relationship with the man she loves. Yes, our gay husbands killed it so we are afraid to ask for the "normal" part of a marriage—namely physical intimacy. We learned to mute our desires for sexual love and the emotional intimacy that goes along with it because it wasn't coming our way unless we "begged" or "groveled." It was easier to give up than to fight this losing battle. This puts a damper on seeking future relationships because we are scared, embarrassed, or fearful of rejection after living with it for so long.

Many of these husbands label themselves "bisexual" while they are married to you. It was easy for them to justify this "fake label" because they "have/had a wife." As my readers know, I don't believe in male "bisexuality." I acknowledge that perhaps there is a handful, but too often this is an excuse used by gay men who don't want to tell the truth. Unless they are making passionate love to their wives on a regular basis, please don't use that word with me. If someone is truly a "bisexual," he can remain loyal to his wife, treat her with sexual passion, and stay away from men. I don't care if they keep their fantasies inside their heads, but not in the bedroom. I don't see that happening hardly ever. Actually, I've never seen it at all. But that's me.

I have been accused by my enemies of destroying good marriages. Ha, ha. Ha. I have to laugh. Women don't come to me to find out how to save their marriages. By the time they contact me, they already explored those options with hopeful sounding groups that call themselves "Mixed Orientation Marriage" groups. I am the leader of the ***Mis-Marriage" group***—the one who acknowledges the marriage was a **MISTAKE** and **needs to end**. I give no false hope. No woman will EVER come back and ask me why I gave her any false hope so she could waste more time in her life fighting a hopeless battle. You can't fix this mistake except for divorce. Gay husbands do **NOT** belong with straight wives. **PERIOD.**

That being said, I also never tell women what to do. They have to make that decision on their own. Sometimes it takes time until a woman can accept that her marriage is doomed. No pressure from me. I just let her know I'm always here for support when she is ready.

Are all women ready at some point? The answer to this is NO. A smaller number of women choose to remain in their marriage to a gay man for a variety of reasons. Fear is one. Finances are another one. Lacking self-confidence to live alone is a third one. I do understand their decision. They are afraid of changing the status quo. They are willing to sacrifice their potential happiness and peace of mind just to exist. They have learned to ask for little or rather nothing because that's what they will get as far as physical affection or intimacy, or they find outside activity to fulfill that need. I don't get it—but I also don't judge it. I learned long ago they every woman exists and walks through life however she can. But these women don't need my help because I cannot in good conscience help someone stay in this kind of destructive situation.

I always say that a woman has to be emotionally free before she can be physically free. A few women in my network are still with their gay husbands, but they are on the road to freedom and need support to get there.

If you are a woman whose life has been shattered by a gay husband and you need support, I am here for you. Write to me at **Bonkaye@aol.com**.

<u>Bonnie Kaye's additional support:</u>

Bonnie's weekly podcasts can be heard at the following link:

http://www.blogtalkradio.com/bonnielkaye

You can purchase Bonnie's other life-saving books on her website at:

www.gayhusbands.com

You can also sign up for her free newsletter on her website and ask for back issues.

www.ingramcontent.com/pod-product-compliance
Lightning Source LLC
Chambersburg PA
CBHW031257090426
42742CB00007B/498